NATIVE AMERICAN

CRAFT INSPIRATIONS

NATIVE AMERICAN CRAFT INSPIRATIONS

by Janet and Alex D'Amato

Illustrations by Janet D'Amato

Designed by Alex D'Amato

M. EVANS & COMPANY, INC.   NEW YORK

Library of Congress Cataloging-in-Publication Data

D'Amato, Janet.
    [American Indian craft inspirations]
    Native American craft inspirations / by Janet and Alex D'Amato ; illustrations by Janet D'Amato ;
designed by Alex D'Amato.
        p. cm.
    Previously published as: American Indian craft inspirations. 1972.
    Includes index.
    ISBN 0-87131-707-9 : $11.95
        1. Indian craft.   2. Indians of North America—Costume and adornment.   3. Indians of North America—
Art.   4. Indians of North America—Industries.   I. D'Amato, Alex.   II. Title.
    TT157.D34 1992
    745.5—dc20   92-35721
                                                                                                                    CIP

1992

M. Evans and Company, Inc.
216 East 49th Street
New York, New York 10017

Manufactured in the United States of America

9   8   7   6   5   4   3   2   1

*Dedicated to my mother, Florence Cowles Potter,
for her inspiration, encouragement and unstinting help.
Constant creative activity is her way of life and a
priceless inheritance for me. Her talent for so
many crafts (some learned from the Indians) has
contributed so much to this book.*

J.P.D.

Contents

Foreword

This book seeks its inspirations from the past, creating crafts related to our newly awakened interest in the heritage of our continent. This interest is paradoxically an outgrowth of the technological era. For, as change in our life styles accelerates, our desire for some sort of hold on the past becomes increasingly intense. As machines leave us with almost no essential manual work, our need to create with our hands grows proportionally. The exploration of our American Indian cultures satisfies both needs: it uncovers the basic roots of this country, and it reveals unique and functional techniques which can be the inspiration for modern crafts.

In this era of plastic and steel, when everything is mass produced, there is a new yearning for basic creativity. When all the objects we possess have been purchased for money, our relationship to the acquired object remains remote. Our only personal involvement is that we have exercised our taste and judgment in the selection. For many of us this is not enough. We need to experience the kind of pride in our possessions that comes when we have a stake in their creation.

Many fine artists today are deliberately turning to crafts and working with natural or "found" materials. In this respect, the Indians are an ideal source of inspirations for they made creative use of all that surrounded them. Whatever grew or occurred naturally became their raw materials. They used and reused everything, adding an instinctive sense of rhythm and design. What we call crafts, to the Indian, were basic means of making all that was necessary for his existence.

Time and machine-made products have deprived us of the direct relationship with raw materials that the Indians knew. The most we can hope for is a reminder of what they did—that's what this book is about. Inspired by their techniques and excited by their artistry, we have designed a book of purely contemporary crafts. As you create something of your own, we hope it will help you relate and give you the satisfaction of a new connection with our remarkable heritage.

Notes on Materials

Many projects in this book can be made with materials purchased from local stores. Look in variety, department, fabric, and hardware stores for parts to buy. Some projects utilize familiar household items. Craft and artist's supply stores have most of the specialized craft needs. Mail order houses for crafts carry a large range of materials, and simply looking at the catalogue can often inspire a project. In the back of this book some mail order supply houses are listed, with notations on special supplies they carry.

Glue, scissors, a felt tip marker, ruler, tape measure, rags, and masking tape are essential for any crafts work. You should also have at hand a few basic tools such as a knife, a coping saw, an awl, and small pliers. Some of these basic tools are shown on the opposite page. Other useful (but not absolutely necessary) tools are also shown.

Some workshop tools will be needed for certain projects. Basically a hammer, files, hand drill, sandpaper, and vise are needed. Specific tools will be mentioned with each project as they are needed.

For holding things together, white glue (Elmer's or Add-A-Grip) and household cement (Duco) serve most purposes. For stronger bonds, epoxy glues are good. The latter come in two tubes that need mixing; follow the package instructions. White glues such as Tacky or Sobo are ideal for working on fabric, styrofoam and a variety of materials. They will be referred to as "fabric glue" but will serve many purposes. Check the labels to find the materials for which they are best suited. New glues for specific purposes are becoming available; check with your local hardware store for advice on gluing special materials.

As for paints, acrylic paints are usually suggested since they thin with water but dry permanently. All art supply and many variety stores carry artist's acrylic paints. Water colors (poster paints) can be substituted if the finished work is covered with a varnish or a clear plastic finish. There are many kinds of finishes available.

Any plain paper can be used for making patterns. Onion skin or tracing paper (available in art supply stores) is best for tracing designs. For transferring the pattern to cardboard, blacken the back of the tracing paper with an ordinary pencil, place it on the cardboard blackened side down, and re-trace the design. If transferring the design to fabric, use transfer

For most all crafts:

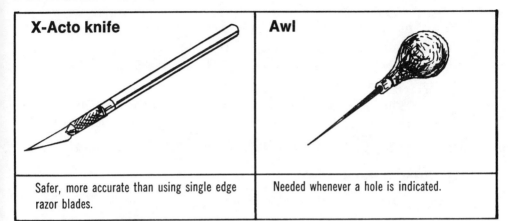

X-Acto knife

Safer, more accurate than using single edge razor blades.

Awl

Needed whenever a hole is indicated.

For many crafts:

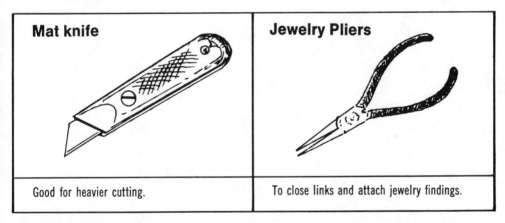

Mat knife

Good for heavier cutting.

Jewelry Pliers

To close links and attach jewelry findings.

For special crafts:

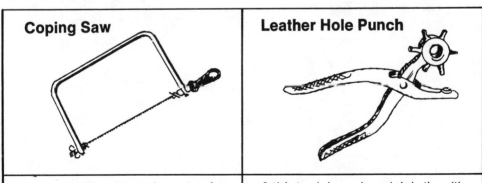

Coping Saw

This saw would be adequate for most sawing of small projects.

Leather Hole Punch

Satisfactory holes can be made in leather with an awl, but this is suggested if a lot of leather work is involved.

sheets and a tracing wheel, both of which are sold in all notions and fabric stores.

Preceding the actual instructions for each project will be a list of special materials and tools needed for that project. Ordinary items that are usually around the house—a ruler, pencil, paper, scissors, thread, needles, pins, rags, tape, and clip clothespins—will not be mentioned.

When you choose a project to make, read it over. Read not only the list of materials, but also the *complete* instructions for making it. Get the whole picture, gather the materials, and then go to it!

To Enlarge Patterns

In some cases, squared areas are given for enlarging patterns or designs. When they are not, make your own grid. Lay a piece of thin paper over design chosen and trace outline. Draw on a grid (½″ squares is a good size, ¼″ if design is very small.)

On another sheet of paper draw a larger grid. (To double size of a drawing with ½″ grid, make new grid of 1″ squares). Now draw outline on the larger grid using small grid for guide, counting corresponding squares as necessary. This enables you to get proper proportions in the enlarged drawing.

For other sizes, make a larger grid in proportion to enlargement needed.

12

Pattern or design (size given).

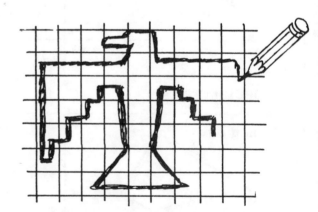

Make larger squares (size indicated on pattern), draw enlarged design.

𝒥EWELRY

The term jewelry covers a vast number of Indian creations: necklaces, pendants, garters, ankle trims and earrings are among the many adornments produced by the various Indian cultures. The design and purpose of the body adornments varied according to the tribe and area. Unmarried daughters of the Pueblo peoples, for example, wore turquoise mosaic pendants in their ears. Bird fetishes carved from shell were strung into necklaces by the Zuni. Beads ground from the quahog, "wampum," were used as money or woven into ceremonial belts.

All kinds of materials were used for jewelry or body adornments. Quills, shell, bone, silver, turquoise and beads were employed in jewelry making. Beads themselves were made of numerous materials, ranging from shell to stone to turquoise.

Since beadworking offers such a variety of creative possibilities, both in the composition of the beads themselves, and in the objects they can be worked into, we'll begin our discussion of jewelry here.

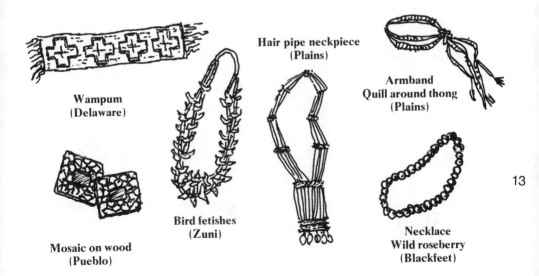

Wampum
(Delaware)

Mosaic on wood
(Pueblo)

Bird fetishes
(Zuni)

Hair pipe neckpiece
(Plains)

Armband
Quill around thong
(Plains)

Necklace
Wild roseberry
(Blackfeet)

13

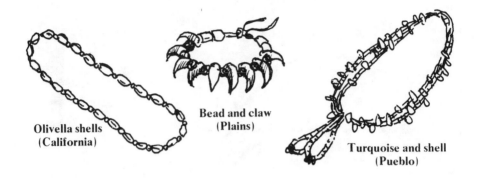

Olivella shells
(California)

Bead and claw
(Plains)

Turquoise and shell
(Pueblo)

History of Beadwork

Bead making is a craft that goes back over a thousand years. Sea shells are one of the oldest bead materials, and were used not only by coastal tribes, but also by those who lived inland, who got them from traders or made the trek themselves to the ocean to seek the shells.

To make beads, the shell is broken into small pieces which are then pierced with a hand drill. The drilled pieces are strung on a cord and "sanded" on a slab of sandstone until they are rounded to the desired diameter.

The most familiar beads perhaps are glass beads which were introduced by the Europeans in the latter part of the seventeenth century. Initially, large, bulky beads of glass and china were used for bracelets, fringe decorations, and other ornaments. By the nineteenth century, beads of about 1/8" diameter were being used for sewn beadwork, but by the end of the century even tinier, "seed" beads had replaced these. The former are now referred to as "real beads" or "E beads."

Indians still make their own beads of shell and stone, but for our purposes glass beads are easier and more accessible. The following guide will give you an idea of what is readily available.

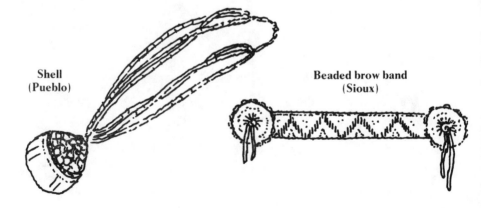

Shell
(Pueblo)

Beaded brow band
(Sioux)

Before Launching Into Beadwork

Commercially Available Beads: Many stores have a bewildering assortment of beads. If ordering by mail from craft suppliers, you should know what you will be getting.

Here is a quick summary of commercially available beads. Each bead shown here is approximately actual size. Some catalogs designate beads by the inch size, others list them in millimeters.

Larger holes are needed when beads are to be strung on cords or on thongs. Beads sold for macramé usually have good size holes. Most wooden beads have large holes, but not all. There are many other kinds of beads used for stringing, but the ones listed are the most commonly available in stores or from craft supply catalogs.

SMALL HOLES

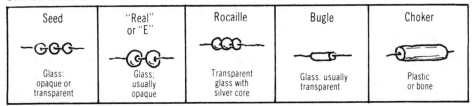

Seed	"Real" or "E"	Rocaille	Bugle	Choker
Glass: opaque or transparent	Glass; usually opaque	Transparent glass with silver core	Glass: usually transparent	Plastic or bone

LARGE HOLES

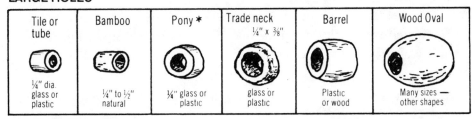

Tile or tube	Bamboo	Pony *	Trade neck ¼" x ⅜"	Barrel	Wood Oval
¼" dia. glass or plastic	¼" to ½" natural	¼" glass or plastic	glass or plastic	Plastic or wood	Many sizes — other shapes

HOLES VARY IN SIZE

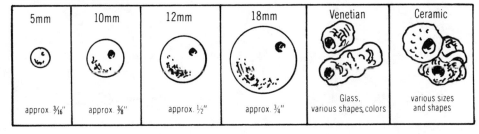

5mm	10mm	12mm	18mm	Venetian	Ceramic
approx. ³⁄₁₆"	approx. ⅜"	approx. ½"	approx. ¾"	Glass, various shapes, colors	various sizes and shapes

＊"Pony" is a popular name for this bead, but dealers who use more authentic Indian terms call this and a slightly larger bead "trade-neck" or "crow" bead. To them the "pony" bead is the E size.

Homemade Beads: You can make beads yourself of homemade clay as the Mexican and Central American Indians did. Combined with purchased beads they give a special handmade look to necklaces.

There are many kinds of self-hardening clays, both homemade and commercial. Ask your craft supply or art store dealer for advice concerning the best one for your needs. Some of these clays harden in air, others can be set by heating in a home oven.

The Central and South American Indians still make clay out of bread —a technique that you can readily adapt. Remove the crust from a slice of bread. Add 1 tablespoon of white glue for each slice. Wet tips of the fingers with a little detergent and start kneading. It's very sticky at first. Gradually the glue is absorbed and it becomes a fine grain, workable, modeling medium. If you want color add some food dye or acrylic paint and knead through.

Shape the beads for stringing. Not all beads need to be spherical. Try various other shapes (Fig. 1).

Press on a bumpy surface for textured effect (Fig. 2), if desired.

To form the necessary hole, cut open one end of a wire coat hanger, and push on a bead (Fig. 3). Or use a toothpick to make the hole. Repeat with each bead. Allow to dry, or put in a "low" oven (with the door open) to speed up drying.

For greater variety in color the beads can be painted when dry. There are several craft materials that give a glaze-like finish. Inquire at your craft or art supply dealer.

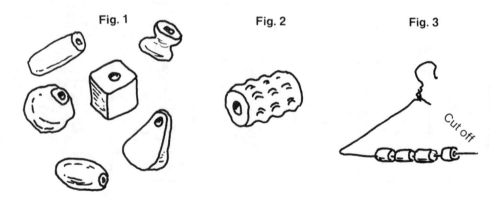

Fig. 1   Fig. 2   Fig. 3

Cut off

Alternate Bead Sources—Second Hand: Old jewelry is an excellent source for unusual bead shapes as well as for chains, links, and clasps. Delve into rummage sales, garage sales, second hand shops. Parts of old necklaces can be used. Select with an eye toward the uses of individual beads. Old brooches and earrings can often be disassembled to get beads. *Practice with Pasta:* Before investing in beads you might like to become familiar with beading techniques using substitutes. Pasta can be used to make some fun-fake ornaments, but it does not make solid jewelry. Tubettini macaroni is a good size for stringing and works best when combined with a few large beads (Fig. 4).

Dip macaroni in cold dye briefly—do not soak it. Dry thoroughly and string gently, as they are not as sturdy as real beads.

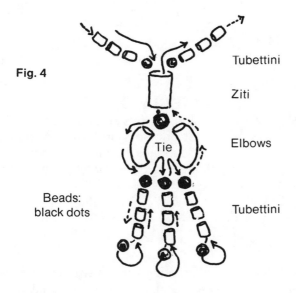

Fig. 4

Tubettini

Ziti

Tie   Elbows

Beads:
black dots   Tubettini

Stringing: For stringing beads with fine holes (seed and some decorative beads) you need a beading needle and fine sturdy thread. Nylon fishing line or beading wire can be used without a needle.

For stringing beads with larger holes, any of the following could be used: cord, string, thong, yarn. Nylon fishing line is unbreakable and practical for all size holes.

Simple stringing can create exciting jewelry: from multistrands of tiny seed beads to dramatic necklaces of chunky beads.

17

Pueblo Necklaces

Old necklaces made by the Pueblo peoples of Arizona and New Mexico were made of stone and shell. Holes were drilled in fragments of various sizes. Then these pieces were strung. The fragments were rounded into beads by rubbing them on sandstone.

These traditional necklaces have two strands of beads hanging down in front. There is a belief that once these two strands were earrings. When an Indian was working at daily chores he could remove the earrings and attach them to his necklace. At other times, they were worn as earrings. Gradually over the generations the two strands became a permanent part of the necklace.

Make yourself a necklace of this design by combining handmade and purchased beads.

MATERIALS
Beads, various sizes and shapes in color or colors preferred (or handmade beads), including about 20 elongated ones; nylon fishing line.

String beads on fishing line, alternating various size beads in random sequence and occasionally inserting elongated beads. Make a string about 27″ long.

For dangles, make a string of tile beads about 8″ long, with three larger beads in center. Tie, forming a loop. Tie loop around line in center of necklace. Work loop ends up inside necklace beads on either side. Add a dab of glue to secure knot. Repeat for second dangle.

Slide all beads together so no nylon line shows but so that there is sufficient give to keep necklace flexible. Tie at back, dab some glue on knot. Hide ends by slipping into beads on either side. Or if you prefer attach a purchased necklace catch.

18

Bead and Yarn Combination

This method of stringing uses fewer beads. The color of the stringing materials becomes a vital part of the necklace. Here, use any fascinating beads with large holes you choose, keeping in mind that variety makes it more attractive. Use a selective eye to create vibrant color combinations and interesting textural effects.

MATERIALS
Selection of beads with large holes; colorful yarn (2,3 or 4 colors) medium weight; yarn needle (needle threader is helpful); fabric glue.

For stringing, cut four pieces of yarn 45″ long. For finishing ends, cut four pieces of yarn 22″ long, sixteen pieces 6″ long. Yarn can be any combinations of colors desired.

To bead, thread all four 45″ yarn pieces through one needle. Slide beads onto all four strands together. Tie a knot on either side of each bead or group of beads (Fig. 1). Leave yarn showing between. You might choose an arrangement with a repeating sequence of beads. (Fig. 2). String and knot an arrangement that measures about 30″ overall.

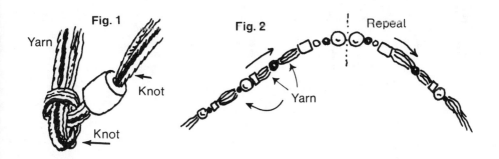

19

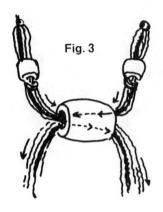

Fig. 3

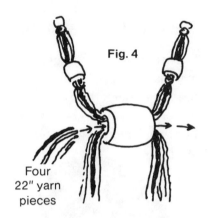

Fig. 4

Four
22" yarn
pieces

For the center of the front, select one large attractive bead with an extra large hole. Put yarn ends through in opposite directions (Fig. 3). To add extra hanging strands in center, thread the four 22" yarn pieces on the needle. Slide through center bead (Fig. 4). There are now four sets of yarn hanging from the center bead.

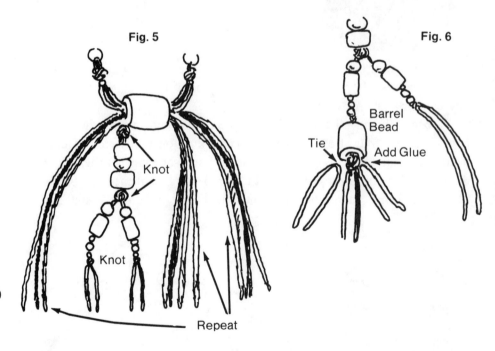

Fig. 5

Knot

Knot

Repeat

Fig. 6

Barrel
Bead

Tie

Add Glue

Slip three beads on each group of four strands, then separate each group into 2 strands and string smaller beads below to each two strands of yarn. Repeat all across making 8 strings of hanging beading (Fig. 5). Knot below last smaller bead so that each "fringe" hangs 3″ below center bead. Lengths should vary slightly.

To finish ends, slide a large-holed bead such as a barrel bead on each strand. Below it, tie on two of the 6″ pieces of yarn. Tie these pieces at their center directly below barrel bead (Fig. 6). Dab glue around this

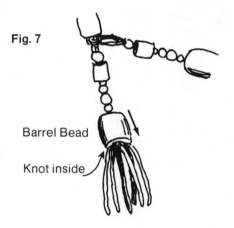

Fig. 7

Barrel Bead

Knot inside

knot and slide the barrel bead down to hide the knot (Fig. 7). This makes a tassel of six yarn strands. Repeat on all eight ends.

Try the necklace on and see how it hangs. Adjust the lengths, if necessary, and trim the ends leaving about 2″ of yarn hanging below last bead.

You can also make a handsome belt. Cut four strands of yarn 55″ long. Omit center bead. Leave ends open to form ties. Finish with four ends (Fig. 8).

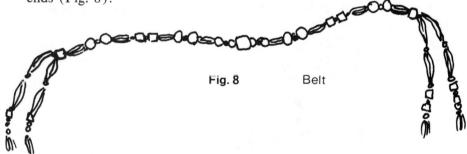

Fig. 8   Belt

Beadwork on a Loom

The Plains Indians were masters of beading on a loom and decorated their clothing, moccasins and personal equipment with this type of beadwork.

Excellent looms are available in craft supply stores, but there is a special satisfaction in making your own. This sturdy loom is quite simple and has many other uses as well.

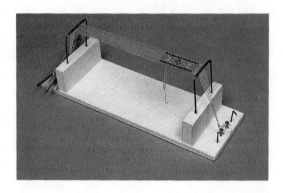

Materials

For loom: Scrap wood, two wire hangers, small wire springs, four cup hooks, six 1½" nails, nylon fishing line, four clip clothespins, two ice cream sticks, white glue, cutting pliers, drill, screwdriver, hammer.

For beading: Seed beads (three or four colors), sheet of graph paper (marked in very small squares), beading needle, thread or very fine nylon line.

The Loom

For the base of the loom, cut a piece of wood about 15" x 4½". Cut two blocks of wood 4½" x 1½" high out of wood about ¾" thick.

Snip off the bases of two fairly sturdy wire hangers to get two pieces of wire each about 9½" long.

Dismantle some old dried-up useless ball point pens. You'll need two springs out of the pens. If you wish to do a wide bead panel, find four such springs.

Now assemble your loom. Glue and nail the blocks to base as shown (Fig. 1).

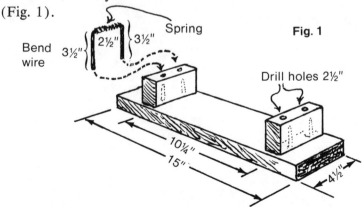

Bend wire 3½" 2½" 3½" 3½" Spring

Fig. 1

Drill holes 2½"

10¼"
15"
4½"

Bend the pieces of wire as shown (Fig. 1). Wire will be inserted into each end block. It will be necessary to drill holes, using either a hand or a power drill. Test the size of the drill on scrap wood to make sure the hole will hold the wire securely. When you have the proper size drill, make holes in both blocks as shown.

Slip one (or two) springs over the wire and slide to center. Insert the bent wire into the hole. Repeat on other end. If wires tend to wobble, remove—apply glue and insert again.

Insert opened cup hooks or screws into ends of board (Fig. 2). These will hold the warp and beading in position.

Ice cream sticks will be clipped onto these.

Your loom is complete. Paint it black or white if you like.

Fig. 2

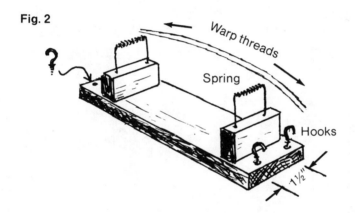

Warp threads
Spring
Hooks
1½"

Beading: The threads on the loom are called the warp. Fishing line makes a sturdy warp. It should not be too heavy (six lbs. or less).

The length of the warp will be determined by the size of the beadwork you plan to make. This loom will make a piece of beadwork about 10" long without moving, but beading can be moved along to make any length. Whatever the length of your beading, each warp thread must be *at least* 26". For beading longer than 10", figure length of finished beaded unit plus an allowance of 8" on each end, to tie into position.

Cut warp threads. A 10-warp piece which takes 9 beads across is a good starting size. Tie the ends in a bundle around one ice cream stick. Place against the hooks and hold with a clothespin (Fig. 3).

23

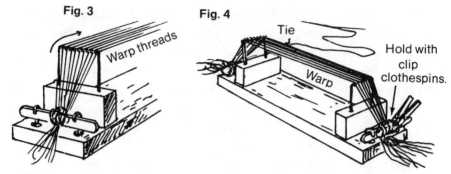

Fig. 3

Warp threads

Fig. 4

Tie

Warp

Hold with clip clothespins.

Pull warp up across the springs and tie to ice cream stick on other end. Space warp evenly, so that each thread is just far enough from the next to accommodate one bead (Fig. 4). After spreading threads, tighten tension, if necessary, at one end. Hold to hooks with clip clothespins. The warp should always be very firm.

Now you are ready to design your beadwork. With graph paper and colored pencils or felt pens, it is easy to plan a meaningful design for yourself.

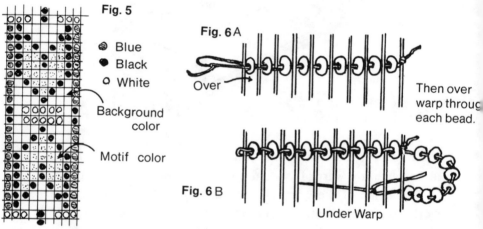

Fig. 5

◓ Blue
● Black
○ White

Background color

Motif color

Fig. 6 A

Over →

Then over warp through each bead.

Fig. 6 B

Under Warp

On a piece of graph paper, mark the color of each bead of a motif (9 beads wide). This motif can be repeated along the bead panel. The motif shown in Fig. 5 has limited colors. You will probably want more. There are many motifs suitable for beadwork. Chose a simple one, with one color predominating for background.

To string beads, use a beading needle and nylon thread or fine fishing line. Tie the beading thread on loom as shown (Fig. 4). String on 9 beads and stretch them across *under* the warp threads. With your left index finger ease each bead into position, one between each warp

24

thread. Push the row of beads up above the warp threads and thread the needle back through each bead (Fig. 6, A-B). This time the weaving thread goes *over* all the warp threads and secures the beads in place.

Repeat, placing the beaded thread underneath the warp, pushing the beads up into position, taking the needle back through beads going over warp threads (Fig. 6). Continue back and forth. Use the graph paper guide to select the proper color beads each time when stringing them on the needle. As each row is finished push it up firmly with the tip of the needle against the previous row.

If you are making a long piece, it will be necessary to move the beading along the loom, to expose more warp thread to work on. Roll the finished work around the ice cream stick, hold with clothespin against wire as well as base hooks. Release enough new thread and retie the warp threads firmly in place to maintain tension.

When you reach the end of the beading thread, or a piece is finished, tie a knot in the weaving thread after the last bead, then weave back through several beads in the adjacent row and cut off. New weaving

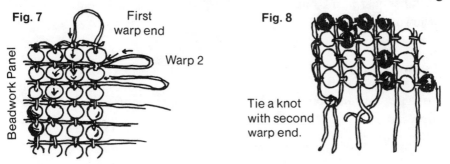

Fig. 7

First warp end

Warp 2

Beadwork Panel

Fig. 8

Tie a knot with second warp end.

thread is started in the same way. Thread through several beads in the last row, knot at side, and continue beading.

To finish the warp threads when beading is complete (Fig. 7), make a knot in the warp thread that is on the outside left, string the warp thread through several beads in the adjacent row. Tie a knot between beads, go through two more beads and cut off. Knot and secure each succeeding warp thread. Each time going through different adjacent beads, working further into beaded panel as necessary.

25

If you plan to sew beading to a fabric, warp threads can be knotted, two together (Fig. 8). Trim to about 1″ below knots. Fold the knotted threads under the piece of beading when you sew it in place.

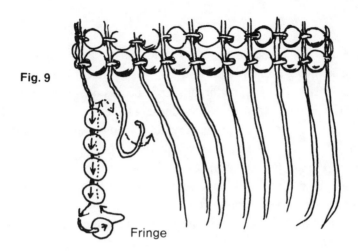

Fig. 9

Fringe

To finish with a beaded fringe, beads are strung on warp ends. On one warp end, string number of beads desired. Thread back into next to the last bead, and through remaining beads (Fig. 9). Pull up firmly against beadwork. Tie end to second warp thread end. Hide both ends by going up through several beads in the beaded panel, cut off. Continue on other warp ends, making five beaded fringe strings on a 10-warp beadwork.

Using Loomed Beadwork

There are many uses for loomed beadwork pieces. Here are a few suggestions:

MATERIALS
Beaded work; plastic bracelet; leather; glue.

Bead and Leather Bracelet: Make a beaded strip about 10¼" long. Remove from loom and tie ends as shown in Figure 8 on previous page. For base, use an old plastic bracelet about ¾" wide. Cut a piece of thin leather about 2" wide x 10¼". Fold leather around plastic and sew (Fig. 1). Make the leather taut.

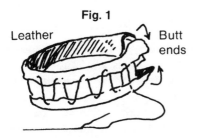

Fig. 1

Leather

Butt ends

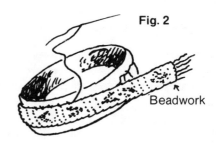

Fig. 2

Beadwork

The ends of the leather must be butted (joined end to end without overlapping) so surface is smooth inside. Butt by trimming the ends of leather, and gluing them firmly to the bracelet.

Fold under the warp threads of one end of beadwork, glue. When dry, sew the beadwork around the bracelet, sewing the edge of the warp to the leather covering. Try to maintain even margins of leather on each side of beading (Fig. 2).

When you have sewn the beadwork completely around the bracelet, you may need to remove a few rows of beads to make beadwork ends butt—or maybe you'll need to add some rows. Beading should fit around the bracelet exactly. When the length of the beaded piece is correct, fold warp ends under and glue. Sew the end rows of beads together. It should now look like a continuous beaded strip.

Other uses: Beadwork panels can be attached wherever you wish. Sew one to a strip of leather or other material for a belt, wristband or choker. Fold back the ends of the beadwork, sew the beaded piece to the material (felt or leather). Attach hook and eye or tap on snap to the felt or leather (Fig. 3). For a belt add a buckle to the material. Glue two beaded panels on a purchased belt (Fig. 4).

The uses for this kind of beadwork are countless. Use your ingenuity to decide where to put it next.

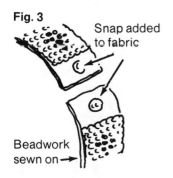

Fig. 3

Snap added to fabric

Beadwork sewn on →

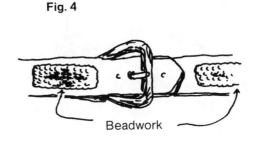

Fig. 4

Beadwork

Direct Beading

A loom is not the only way to create beaded designs. Long before beads became available decorations were made of seeds, quills and other natural materials applied directly to fabric or leather. At first, only a few beads were included in these designs. As beads became more easy to obtain, larger and larger areas were filled in with beadwork. In the 19th century beading reached its height, and a papoose carrier or dress yoke might be completely covered with beading. Such decorations in addition to requiring skill and talent showed great devotion and patience.

Baby Carrier
(Kiowa)

Pipe Bag
(Sioux)

Early beading was done with sinew, without needles. Eventually needles became available in trade to facilitate beading.

Handles and thongs were also beaded. To bead a thong, a thread was knotted on at the top, several beads were strung on and wound tightly around the thong, then secured by sewing through the thong. This procedure was repeated until the thong was completely covered with beads.

For our purposes, we will use two basic methods of applying beads to fabric or leather: the one needle or "direct beading" method, and the two needle method called the "overlaid process." Almost all beading techniques are variations of these. Practice each and you'll quickly understand the method.

The design shown to practice direct beading is a traditional Choctaw design: two circles, connected by a band in a scroll effect.

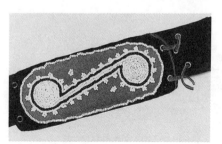

MATERIALS

Seed beads (black or dark blue and white); beading needle; regular sewing needle; 8" square of red felt; 7" embroidery hoop.

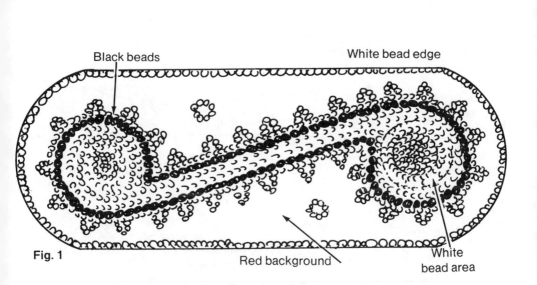

Black beads

White bead edge

Red background

White bead area

Fig. 1

Plan the design (Fig. 1) and lightly draw outline on felt. Stretch the felt in an embroidery hoop—it is easier to work on a firm surface.

The easiest and quickest way to catch seed beads on the needle is to pour a few at a time onto a washcloth or terry potholder. Then they won't roll around as you spear them.

ONE NEEDLE METHOD

Fig. 2

For the circular motif and center lines, use the single needle method (Fig. 2). Thread beading needle, tie knot, bring needle up through fabric, string on three or four beads, sew back down into the fabric following the design. Bring needle up through again as close as possible to last bead and repeat, following design (Fig. 1). Make sure to keep beading flat and close to other beads.

29

TWO NEEDLE METHOD

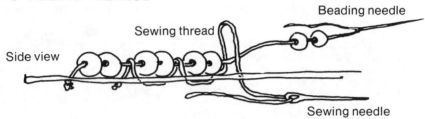

Fig. 3

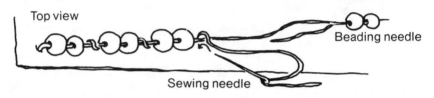

The other direct beading method uses two needles. Try it on the border of this design. This method was often preferred for intricate beadwork.

String beads on a beading needle, lay across the fabric. A second needle, (sewing needle), is brought up from behind, across the thread of the bead string and down into the fabric (Fig. 3). Bring up again between beads further along the string. In diagrams, beads are slightly separated to show sewing process. In actual work, the beads lie lightly against each other and the stitches do not show.

The Indians often made the stitches of the second thread go through only the top layer of leather. No stitching showed on back. This was good for moccasins where knots might be uncomfortable.

To finish beading the Choctaw design, make little white loops of beads along the edge of the beaded design. Come up from the back, string on 5 white beads, go back down close to the same spot, creating a beaded loop. Count 7 beads of the beaded edge line, come up for next loop. String on 5 beads and go back down in same spot. Move along 7 beads and repeat (Fig. 4).

Fig. 4   Loop

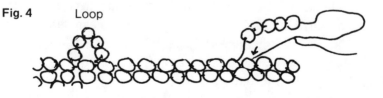

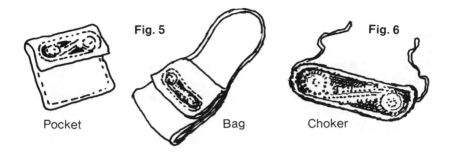

Fig. 5

Fig. 6

Pocket   Bag   Choker

To make sure beading on the edges of the fabric is secure, use fabric glue to secure the outside row of beads to the felt. When dry, trim felt fairly close to beaded edge, being careful not to cut thread.

Now do whatever you like with this beaded motif. Sew or glue it to a surface for decoration. Make two to sew onto pockets or perk up an old belt or bag (Fig. 5).

To make it into a choker, cut a piece of black felt or lightweight suede leather 8½″ x 2¼″ (or size that will fit under beadworked panel). Round corners. Cut two pieces of cord or thong about 7″ long, each. Sew on each side (Fig. 6). Tie in back.

This practice piece gives you an understanding of the direct beadwork technique so that you can do any design. If you need to cover a surface completely with beads, it may be easier to work on a needlework canvas since the threads are counted and lines straight.

All sorts of designs can be adapted for direct beading. For large solidly beaded areas, use the direct method—back and forth. Draw design on graph paper so you know which beads to select as you go across row after row (Fig. 7).

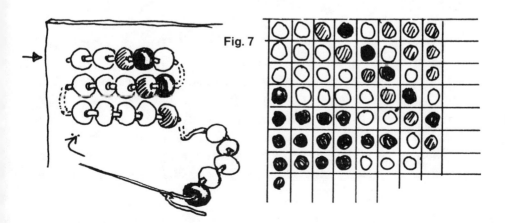

Fig. 7

31

Interwoven Chest Piece

Another beading technique used by the Indians produced a solid beaded unit without any backing and without using a loom.

Using this method, other elements, such as shells, can be successfully combined with the beads. The technique is very old but can be used to create "now" jewelry.

MATERIALS

About 125 round beads about ¼" or ⅜" diameter, all one color or in combinations such as 25 brown, 100 tan; an assortment of smaller beads in harmonizing colors (for fringe of neckpiece); three shells (optional); yarn or cord for stringing; yarn needles; fabric or white glue.

The basic rectangular shape for necklace will be 4 beads high, 8 or 9 beads wide.

To make this bead piece, start at lower right corner. String on 4 beads. Hold firmly (or pin down starting corner so it doesn't twist). Leave 3 inches of string at the beginning. Later a fringe will be strung on it.

String on next bead (bead A), go back into No. 3 bead of those already strung (Fig. 1). String on another bead (B), skip second bead and go back through the No. 1 bead.

Tie a knot firmly below bead No. 1 and start up next row (Fig. 2). String on bead C and go up into bead B. String on a new bead, go back through bead A. The process is simple once you get it started. Pull thread firmly so beads are nestled closely next to each other.

Continue until you have 9 beads across the top row and your last bead is at lower left corner (Fig. 3). Tie end and allow extra to hang down.

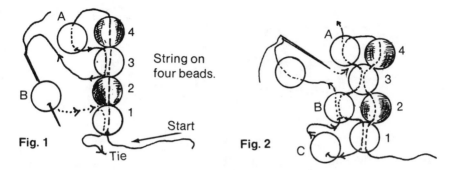

Fig. 1

String on four beads.

Start

Tie

B

A

4 3 2 1

Fig. 2

A

B

C

4 3 2 1

To make fringe, thread a needle on one of the cords hanging from the corner. String on a varied assortment of beads about 2½" long or as long as you like. After last bead, string on a small bead, then go back up into last few beads and tie (Fig. 4). Repeat on the other side.

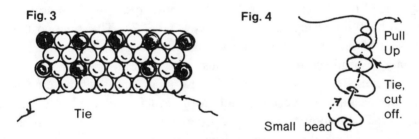

Fig. 3

Tie

Fig. 4

Pull Up

Tie, cut off.

Small bead

Tie on a bead fringe in the center, or if you have some attractive shells available, use them. To hang the shells, cut a piece of string about 6" long. Tie a bulky knot in one end. Saturate knot with glue and pull the knot inside of the shell. Work the knot around the inside so that it doesn't show. With a toothpick dab more glue at the top edge of the shell to secure the cord and assure that the shell will hang properly.

When the glue is thoroughly dry, string on a few assorted beads above the shell, and tie the beaded thread to the beaded panel. String several shells in this manner and tie them to the panel at even intervals. Secure cords by sewing through several beads of the beaded panel and cut off.

To be sure that the fringe is secure, put a dot of glue with a toothpick at each point where you have tied a fringe. Dab in some glue at points where the ends of the fringe were cut and push the ends into the beads to hide and secure.

To make the cord to go around your neck, a string of single beads is sufficient, or tie on a thong.

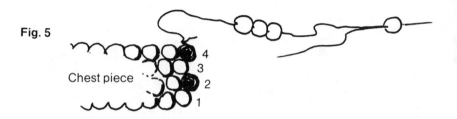

Fig. 5

Chest piece

4
3
2
1

Or you can bead a neckpiece using the same method as the chest piece. Tie the end of the beading thread above the No. 4 bead. Loosely string on 18 beads, (Fig. 5). For second row string on a new bead, and go back into the next to the last strung bead (Fig. 6). String another bead and go into fourth bead from the end (Fig. 6). Continue stringing, going back through alternate strung beads. This is the same procedure as before except you are making a longer string. When you have beaded down the row, tie the cord above bead A of chestpiece. Then go back up, stringing on a third row (Fig. 7). This time go into each bead of the second row, alternating with newly strung bead. Pull up firmly so beads nestle tightly against each other.

Tie at end. Repeat on other side. These loose ends may be used to tie on the necklace or tie these ends to a regular necklace clasp. Use a hook type or a loop type closing. After tying to clasp loop, run the ends of string back through several beads, tie and cut off.

This beading technique can be expanded for any type of article that uses medium or large size beads in a flat area (such as a purse or mat). Once the initial rows are started, it works easily and a piece can be of any size.

Fig. 6

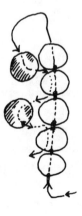

Fig. 7

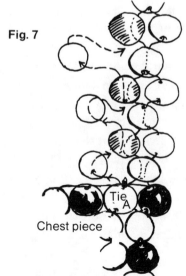

Tie
A

Chest piece

Shells for Jewelry

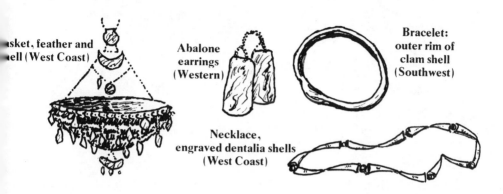

Basket, feather and shell (West Coast)

Abalone earrings (Western)

Bracelet: outer rim of clam shell (Southwest)

Necklace, engraved dentalia shells (West Coast)

Shells are ideal materials for jewelry. The Indians utilized shells in a number of ways. They shaped shell fragments into beads; slices of shell were inlaid into other materials, whole or cut shells decorated garments, baskets and other household articles. Some tribes shaped large shells into practical utensils: cups, spoons and bowls.

The Indians' use of shells was so timelessly creative that it becomes an inspiration even for the most modern jewelry.

Shells with Beaded Tops

Once shells served as dishes—the only ones available. Now, coming full circle, it is possible in this stainless steel era to buy in many hardware stores large scallop shells to be used to cook and serve seafood for special occasions. These shells make good craft material, since they can be transformed easily into jewelry. Some craft supply stores carry scallop shells of especially fine quality.

MATERIALS
Scallop shells about 3" or 4" diameter; assorted beads (mostly turquoise and white); seed beads and slightly larger ("real" beads); some long beads if desired; necklace catch or thong; scrap of felt; fine nylon line; hand drill; epoxy glue. If necessary, orange or yellow acrylic paint.

35

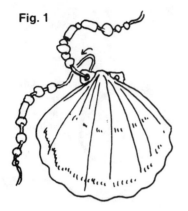

Fig. 1

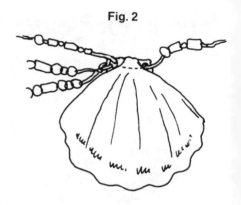

Fig. 2

Prepare shell: If shell is glaringly white, with no natural coloration, tint it lightly. A shell with attractive subtle colors can be used as is.

To tint shell, mix acrylic paint with water until very thin. An orange or yellow color gives the most natural effect. Brush paint over convex surface. Continue to paint and rub off until you get an attractive color.

Drill two holes on either side of the top of the shell.

For stringing the necklace part, use nylon line. String an assortment of beads. Make a string of beads about 7″ long. Go through one of the drilled holes in the top of the shell, bring the line around, tie (Fig. 1). String 7″ more of beads. Tie ends together (Fig. 2). Repeat on other side.

For a third string on each side, string on 7″ of beads, go into hole on left, pass thread under center top of shell, bring thread out other hole (Fig. 2). String on 7″ more of beads.

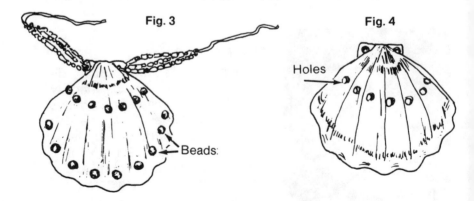

Fig. 3

Beads:

Fig. 4

Holes

36

At each end tie the end of the third strand to the ends of the other two strands. Attach the three strands on one side to one half of a jewelry clasp. Attach the other half of the jeweled clasp to the other side. Beaded ends can be sewn to cord or thong (Fig. 3), if you don't want to use a jewelry clasp.

To decorate the shell, glue on beads using household cement or epoxy. Attach beads in the ridges of shell (Fig. 3), following its natural graceful contours. For neatness, use a toothpick to dab on a tiny bit of glue where needed.

Another way to decorate this same type of shell: after coloring shell (before tying on the necklace), drill a row of holes horizontally between each ridge about 2" down from the top (Fig. 4), curving them to follow the shape of the shell. Put beading wire through one hole from back. String on about 2" of blue beads of varying sizes. Bring wire up over top of shell, twist in back. Repeat, beading entire top of shell. To equalize spread in shell, in some rows bead up only part way, go through existing rows of beads at top and pull wire out at top (Fig. 5). Twist all wires around in back.

When complete, wire on a row of beads horizontally, across where holes were drilled. String the bead necklace as before or string shell on a thong (Fig. 6). Glue piece of felt in back to hide wired area.

Certain clam and ark shells could be made up in this manner. Sometimes sections of shells can be found that show interior spirals. These make attractive necklaces or pendants. Wire or glue on only enough beads to bring out the beauty of the shells. An especially attractive specimen can simply hang from a thong or a single strand of beading (Fig. 7).

There are hundreds of interesting and unusual shells to work with (see page 221 for sources of supply). Take your jewelry designing on from here.

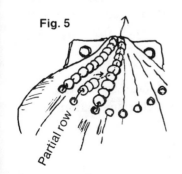

Fig. 5

Partial row

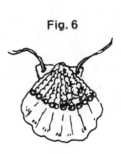

Fig. 6

Fig. 7

Beads

Gorget Shell Etching

Spiro mound

Illinois mound

The pendant below was inspired by a gorget. Originally gorgets were probably worn by warriors for the purpose of protecting the throat during battles. Later they were worn for decorative or ceremonial purposes.

These gorgets were made by engraving fascinating designs on a piece of conch shell. Birds, insects or reptiles were often depicted and some designs represented human figures.

With patience you can make a piece to wear that looks as though it came right out of a museum. If you find it tedious, remember that the Indians used only bone and stone tools.

MATERIALS

4" scallop shell, available in stores for serving seafood (or shell of fresh water clam); thong or cord 24" long; black acrylic paint; dark color wax crayon; coping saw; awl; hand drill.

For ersatz gorget: Clay; plaster of Paris or Durham's Water Putty; black and white acrylic paint; plastic finish such as Gloss polymer medium (available in art store).

Cutting: the gorget is a roughly circular shape. On the inside of shell mark area to be cut off (Fig. 1). Using a coping saw, cut away top of the shell. Go slowly and handle gently to prevent shell from cracking. Drill two holes in top about 1" apart.

For pattern, trace design on paper (Fig. 2).

Rub wax crayon on back of pattern. Tape in position on the concave surface of the shell. With a hard sharp pencil, trace pattern onto shell. Remove pattern.

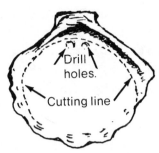

Fig. 1

Drill holes.

Cutting line

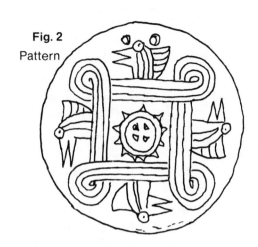

Fig. 2
Pattern

Scratch the design into the surface of the shell with an awl. Scratch lightly, then go over to deepen the grooves. Keep each line fine, don't make any line wider than a single scratch. The lower portion of the shell will probably scratch more easily than the top. Work carefully, trying not to let the awl slip.

When complete, cover the surface with a coat of black acrylic paint and wipe off immediately. Black will remain in the scratched areas. Polish off any black residue on the surface, maintaining the black in the scratched areas. In some areas the scratch may not have been deep enough. Scratch and repeat the staining process. If some spots are too hard to scratch, use a fine brush to paint whatever lines are necessary. Scratch edge of paint to blend into etched lines.

Slip thong or cord through holes (Fig. 3). Wear high on the throat or hanging as a pendant.

Ersatz Gorget: If you prefer not to work with real shells, it is possible to make an easy ersatz gorget.

First make a molded plaster disk. Use child's modeling clay for a mold, making a 4″ circle with a lip (Fig. 4). Mix a little plaster of paris

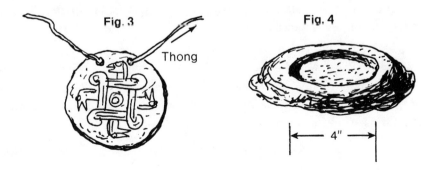

Fig. 3

Thong

Fig. 4

4″

39

(or putty), in a disposable cup, to thick cream consistency. Pour into the clay mold, a little less than ¼ " in depth. Allow to set. Remove from the mold and allow to become nearly dry. Sand surface and drill two holes carefully in the top. Transfer the woodpecker design tracing as before. To scratch design, surface should be hard, but not completely dry. If the surface is too wet, the lines will not be crisp; if too dry, it may not scratch well.

To finish, fill in scratches with black as before. This time, however, black will not wipe off surface cleanly. To get a clean surface, paint over surface with white paint, going around black etched lines. Complete with a coat of clear plastic finish. String on a cord.

Shell Fragments for Neckwear

There are jewelry treasures waiting for you on the beach—but you have to be able to spot their potential. Interesting broken fragments of shell can make attractive adornments. A special bonus is that the sea and sand have done all the polishing for you.

This bead and shell combination hangs from a choker—an attractive arrangment that saves on beads.

MATERIALS
Velvet ribbon 20" long, ¼" wide (or soft leather strip); assorted beads: seed, small wood, crow, etc; two attractive fragments of shell about 2" or 2½" long, about ¾" wide, and thick enough not to crack or crumble; three smaller bead-shaped shell fragments (if you find them); fine nylon fishline; drill.

To prepare shells: Smooth off any rough spots with sandpaper, but do try to find pieces naturally rounded and smooth. With the drill, make holes as shown (Fig. 1).

For stringing: Cut a piece of nylon line 24″ long and thread through a needle. Sew this line into ribbon (Fig. 2) at point A. Pull it through the ribbon so that you have two strands of line hanging down. Center the strands so even amounts hang down. Remove needle.

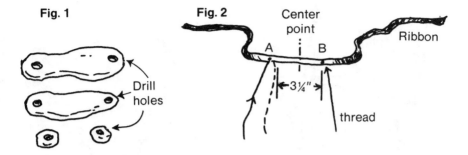

Fig. 1

Drill holes

Fig. 2

Center point

A B

Ribbon

←3¼″→

thread

Start stringing beads, slipping them over both strands of line (Fig. 3). Be careful to hold ends as beads will easily slip off the line. Mix seed beads, "real" beads, etc. in any pleasant combinations of colors and shapes. About ¾″ down slip four seed beads on a single strand, and four on the other strand. Then slip a larger bead over both strands again (Fig. 3). Push up so strand is solidly beaded. Continue this way for about 5½″, occasionally making the double rows of seed beads as shown.

To attach shell, string several seed beads on each strand, (depending how far the hole is from the edge of the shell), slip one strand through the hole from behind, the other strand through same hole from front (Fig. 4). Strands will cross inside hole. Pull down so that seed beads cover most of the strands around shell. Add more seed beads until strands are long enough to meet below shell. Slip a large bead below on both strands.

Add about 1″ more of beads below last large bead. Then repeat the same beading process going through the hole on left side of the second shell fragment.

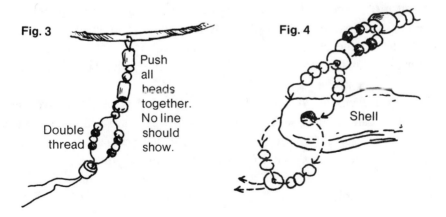

Fig. 3

Push all beads together. No line should show.

Double thread

Fig. 4

Shell

41

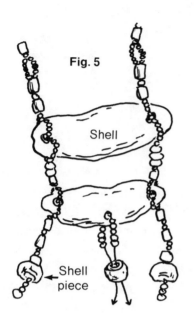

Fig. 5

Shell

Shell piece

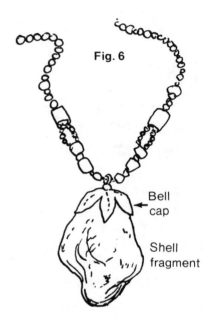

Fig. 6

Bell cap

Shell fragment

To make a bead fringe, bead below the second shell for about 1″. Slip on a small bead-like drilled shell piece (if desired)—add a few more beads then a small bead. Tie ends around small bead, work ends back up through several beads, tie and cut off. A dab of glue at tip and at knot is good insurance it will never come apart.

Start other side by sewing the second piece of nylon line through the ribbon at point B (Fig. 2). Then match the beading arrangement that you have already strung, repeating the process for adding shells. Make a fringe and tie the line off.

Put a 6″ piece of the line through the center hole of the second shell (Fig. 5). Slip on a few seed beads on each strand until the strands meet below the shell. Thread a larger bead over both strands. Add enough beads to match hanging fringe on either side. Tie off as before and necklace is complete.

Fragment Pendant: If you hesitate to drill holes, an attractive shell fragment can be hung, using a bell cap. Bell caps are available in most craft supply stores. It is made of soft metal that you can fit to the contour of the fragment of shell (or stone or whatever you'd like to hang). Glue the cap in position (Fig. 6), using epoxy glue. Put a jump ring through the hole in top and attach to the necklace or cord.

Abalone Inlay

Beaver, carved of wood inlaid with abalone shell. A Tsimshian headdress without ermine trim and bristle crown.

There is a special iridescence in the abalone shell found in no other material. The Indians along the Northwest coast knew how to cut and polish the shell to bring out the fascinating color. They used it on masks, ceremonial hats, and household goods as well as body ornaments. The abalone's delicate color was usually complemented by inlaying it into wood or combining it with leather.

The wood and abalone combination makes effective modern jewelry. Craft shops may carry irregular pieces of abalone. Some mail order suppliers have thin strips for inlaying. Others have bags of fragments of these shells (see page 221). These shell fragments have usually been processed in a rock tumbler which rounds the edges and polishes the surface.

MATERIALS

Polished bits of abalone shell (or inlay strips); pieces of wood about ¼" thick; jewelry findings: pin back, bell cap, pair of earring backs, jump links, etc; coping saw; hand drill; sandpaper; epoxy glue; spray-on varnish or clear plastic coating; brown wood stain.

43

Small scraps of wood are needed. You may find some at a lumberyard or from the discards of home workshop. Mail order craft suppliers carry a variety of woods (page 221). Some have wooden squares and circles (buttons) which you may be able to use without cutting if it suits the shape of your abalone (Fig. 1). Almost all craft supply shops carry balsa wood which is very light (good for earrings especially) and very easy to cut. But it is not as durable nor does it stain and polish as well as the better woods. Exotic woods make up into lovely jewelry, but may need stronger tools.

Tumbled shapes: To make jewelry of tumbled shell pieces sort out abalone shapes. Put aside any similar matching shapes. (Save these for earrings). Select an interesting piece to inlay. Or plan a grouping of several tiny pieces of similar color and thickness. Lay piece (or pieces) on paper and trace around the shape.

Draw an outline for wood shape. Plan a free form that goes well around the abalone shell outline, drawing several until you get a nice balance and size (Fig. 2). When satisfied, transfer outline to wood. With a coping saw, cut the wood into this shape.

Transfer drawing of abalone shape onto the wood shape. To inlay, carve out a space sufficient in area and depth to accomodate the abalone shell piece. With a knife or razor blade make tiny V-shaped cuts into the wood (Fig. 3). A hand drill may be helpful in cutting rounded corners. Drill gently to depth of inlay making sure it only goes part way through.

44

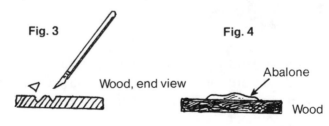

Fig. 5

Indentation
For shell

Wood burned
Decorative line

Keep trying in the shell piece as you work to determine shape and depth of indentation to cut. It does not have to be too deep because the abalone can protrude above wood surface (Fig. 4).

Tools for wood carving or wood cuts are helpful, should you happen to have them. There are even miniature electric roto tools, but they are not necessary for the slight carving needed here.

To Finish Wood: Gently sand entire piece thoroughly with fine sandpaper. Most woods will need staining, depending on the type of wood. Deep brown tones are best to show up the colors of the shell. Brush the stain on or dip the piece into the stain. Let the stain set briefly, then wipe off the excess. After about 15 minutes wipe again and polish to bring out grain of the wood.

A deeper color or an extra design can be etched on the wood with a woodburning tool, if desired. Gently rub the heated tool over the surface to deepen color. Use the tip of tool to burn a darker (Fig. 5) design on the surface. On soft wood, this tool can be used to burn the indentation for inlay.

To complete the finish of the wood, spray on a plastic or varnish coating.

To attach the shell to the wood, use epoxy glue. Fit the shell piece into the indentation as planned. Hold with clip clothespin or a "C" clamp.

Flat Inlay Shapes: If you are inlaying abalone strips, you can use wooden pieces in more angular shapes. Lay the shell on the wood and cut along the shell edge to establish the outline. Cut down into the wood about $\frac{1}{16}$". Or the shape can be cut out of a thin veneer with a knife. Glue the veneer piece to the wood backing. Sand the edges even, stain the wood and glue in the shell strip (Fig. 6). If the abalone needs some polishing, use fine emery cloth or pumice.

45

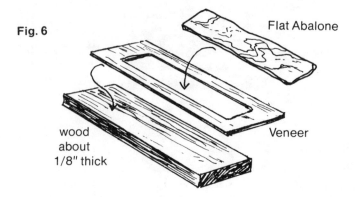

Fig. 6

Flat Abalone

wood
about
1/8" thick

Veneer

Use jewelry findings to assemble either type of inlay. If you are making a pendant, drill a hole in the top of the wood and slip in a jump link to attach a cord, thong or chain. For a brooch or tie pin, use epoxy glue to attach a pin or clip to the back of the piece.

For linked units such as dangle earrings, bracelet or necklace dangles, attach one of the jewelry findings shown in Figure 7. Or you can make a loop by cutting the head off an ordinary straight pin. With narrow tipped pliers, form a loop at the end of the pin. Poke a hole in the top of the wood piece with an awl, add glue to the pin tip and insert the pin (Fig. 8). Add jump links to attach any of these units to each other or to a chain.

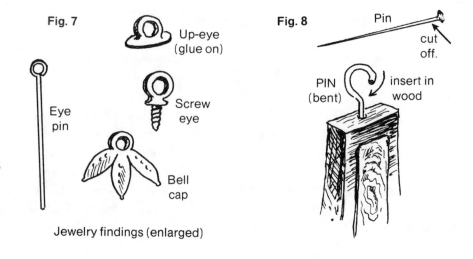

Fig. 7

Up-eye
(glue on)

Eye
pin

Screw
eye

Bell
cap

Jewelry findings (enlarged)

Fig. 8

Pin

cut
off.

PIN
(bent)

insert in
wood

46

SUGGESTED SHAPES FOR TUMBLED ABALONE INLAYS

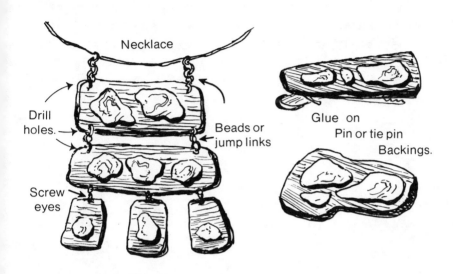

Necklace

Drill holes.

Beads or jump links

Screw eyes

Glue on Pin or tie pin Backings.

SUGGESTED SHAPES FOR FLAT ABALONE INLAYS

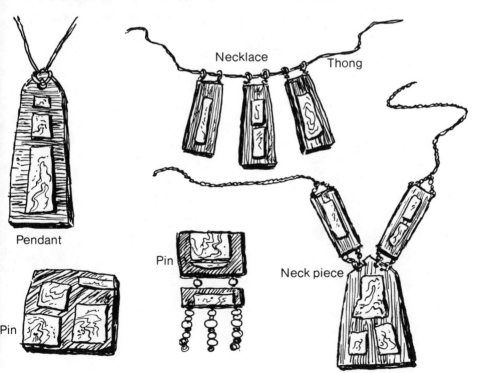

Pendant

Pin

Pin

Necklace

Thong

Neck piece

47

Matching earrings can be made simply by attaching shell pieces to earring backs with epoxy glue (Fig. 9). For dangle type earrings, attach bell caps (available from jewelry supplies), to the abalone piece. Press the cap to fit around the shell, then use epoxy to attach it (Fig. 10). When the glue is dry, attach the shell to the earring back with jump rings. For dangles with inlay-in-wood, use up-eyes or loops (Fig. 11).

The shape of the abalone pieces will determine your design, whatever jewelry you wish to make.

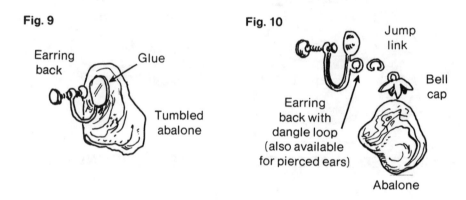

Fig. 9

Earring back
Glue
Tumbled abalone

Fig. 10

Jump link
Bell cap
Earring back with dangle loop (also available for pierced ears)
Abalone

EARRINGS

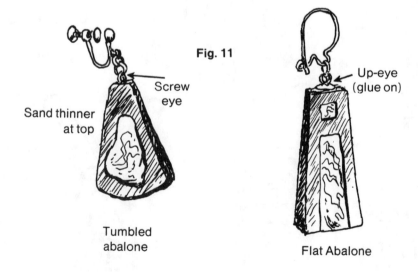

Fig. 11

Screw eye
Sand thinner at top
Tumbled abalone

Up-eye (glue on)
Flat Abalone

Jewelry of Metals

Copper
(Mounds)

Navaho

Zuni

Silverwork and turquoise

Hopi

Although metal was not used frequently by the Indians, some remarkably beautiful pieces of metalwork have been found. It is believed that copper was first worked around Lake Superior where copper nuggets were easily found.

Some of the earliest metal artifacts we have are beautiful ornaments of hammered copper. In the South, particularly Florida, ancient gold ornaments have been discovered, and there are some extremely rare examples of silver from very early cultures, but copper was the single most important metal until the 19th century.

The famous silver jewelry of the Southwest was a craft perfected in recent times. For centuries jewelry had been shaped of turquoise, shell, clay and wood. Around 1850 the Indians started using the Spanish silver coins to make ornaments. This early jewelry was created by hammering the coins into shape. Later came more intricate jewelry techniques, particularly casting, and the addition of turquoise stones.

Navaho jewelry is massive, with only a few accents of turquoise. The most famous Navaho silverwork is the squash blossom necklace and concho belt.

The Zuni use much more turquoise, often covering the entire piece with inlays of stones, or making mosaics of the blue on silver. The Hopi use little or no turquoise to ornament the silver.

Wrist Band

Ancient leather or metal wrist bands probably had a very practical purpose — to protect the archer's arm. Gradually the wrist band evolved into a decorative accessory. Here is a fake silver concoction that can look pretty impressive.

MATERIALS

Piece of suede leather about 2½" x 8"; small ½" buckle (from an old sandal) or buy a "kilt tab" in notions and remove the buckle; *aluminum* can (soda or beer); a variety of beads; beading wire; tin snips (or old scissors); chisel; epoxy and fabric glue.

49

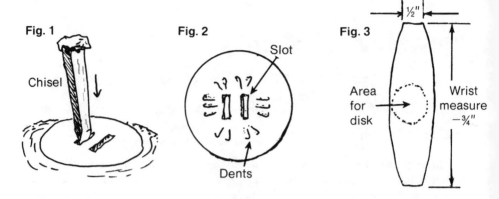

Fig. 1 — Chisel

Fig. 2 — Slot / Dents

Fig. 3 — ½" / Area for disk / Wrist measure —¾"

For "silver" disk, use bottom of the can. Cut off the top and sides with tin snips. Then carefully cut around the bottom, removing the rim. This disk is round and slightly domed. Trim edges evenly.

To make slots, lay disk, dome side down, on a scrap of wood covered with a few layers of rags. Mark off two 1″ long slots about ½″ apart. With hammer and chisel cut these slots (Fig. 1). Fold back extra aluminum and hammer flat.

If you want an embossed effect, hammer the end of a screw driver into the surface of the aluminum without cutting it. Hammer the dents in whatever pattern you chose (Fig. 2).

Turn the disk over. String beads on beading wire alternating silver and turquoise beads. Make a row long enough to go around the outside edge of the disk. With epoxy, glue the beaded wire to the edge, hiding edge. String another row of beads to go inside first row. Glue in place.

To make the wrist band, draw a pattern for the band on paper. The width at center point should be about 2″ to accommodate disk. For length, measure wrist, make length ¾″ less than this measurement. Taper sides down to ½″ (Fig. 3). Fold pattern in half to make sure both sides are alike. Cut out and try on wrist.

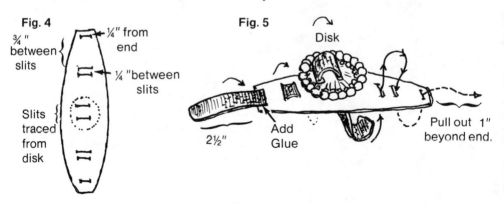

Fig. 4 — ¾″ between slits / ¼″ from end / ¼″ between slits / Slits traced from disk

Fig. 5 — Disk / 2½″ / Add Glue / Pull out 1″ beyond end.

Use this pattern, unfolded, to cut shape out of leather. Cut another strip of leather ½" wide. Determine length by adding 3" to wrist measure. This strip will be laced through the leather shape you have already cut.

Lay disk on leather shape. Try on wrist, bend disk slightly to fit wrist contour.

To lace leather strip into leather shape, it is necessary to cut slits in the shaped leather. Make marks on leather to match slits in disk. Remove disk. Mark other slits ½" long about ¼" apart as shown (Fig. 4). Lay on scrap cardboard and cut slits with knife. Round off the ends of leather strip.

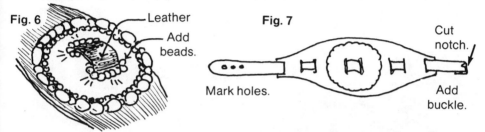

Fig. 6 —Leather · Add beads.

Fig. 7 Cut notch. Mark holes. Add buckle.

To assemble, weave strip into leather shape, up to center slits (Fig. 5). Add some fabric glue to back of the disk, position it on the leather and weave strip through leather up through disk, through the leather to back, then weave up through other slits on band. Position strip as shown (Fig. 5), leaving 2½" at one end. Add a dab of fabric glue, at both ends where strip goes over tips of shaped leather (Fig. 5). Let dry.

For center decoration, wire a few beads and attach to either side of disk where the leather fits through. Slip wire ends under the leather. Add a dab of glue to hold (Fig. 6).

Position buckle and mark spot needed for the tongue. Fold one end of the strip back ¼" (Fig. 7). Cut a tiny notch (or use a leather punch to make a hole). Insert buckle in position through the notch, fold back ends and glue. Cut three notches or punch holes in other end of strip (Fig. 7).

"Silver" disks like this, attached with leather, can be adapted for many things. Use them to decorate a bag. A row of disks can make a belt. Attach a row of smaller disks to a narrower but longer band to make a choker.

Embossed Copper Pendant

Copper was virtually the only metal worked in North America until the Europeans came. The earliest use of copper—dating from around 5,000 B.C. —was for making tools. Later tribes used copper for ornaments, earrings, bracelets and other jewelry.

The Indians worked copper by hammering nuggets into sheets and incising them with bone or stone tools. To cut the copper sheets into shapes, grooves were made on one side of the sheet, the sheet was then reversed and the grooves were ground off with sandstone. Some pendants of open cutwork have also been found.

With modern tools, copper is extremely easy to work. Once you are familiar with the technique, you can create original copper jewelry of your own. Let's begin by making a pendant.

MATERIALS

4" x 6" piece of sheet copper (about 40 gauge), available in most craft and art supply stores; empty ball point pen; dark brown furniture stain; tin snips; hole punch; copper jewelry findings; scrap of heavy leather about 3" x 5½"; leather thong 21" long; scrap of wood.

On lightweight paper trace the eagle design shown.

To prepare copper, lay piece on old block of wood. Find a fairly smooth rock, one that you can hold easily. Beat the copper with the rock. Keep turning the copper, beating on both sides to keep it flat. Beat until the copper piece is evenly textured.

To transfer design, tape pattern to the copper. With an empty ball point pen, trace through the paper, denting the copper sufficiently to see the contour. Remove paper.

Cut out the shape with tin snips or sturdy old scissors. For V shaped junctures between the feathers (Fig. 1), cut in from each side.

Smooth the edges with a file, if necessary. Beat the edges with the rock a little more to help smooth them.

To emboss, put the eagle shape on several layers of newspaper. With

PATTERN FOR EAGLE DESIGN (actual size)

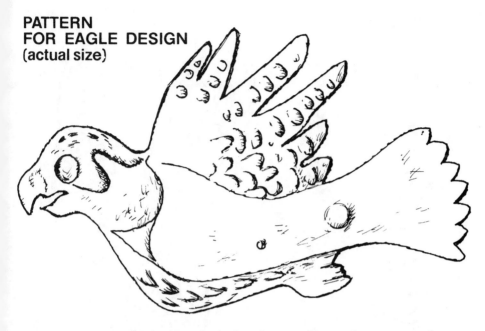

the empty pen, incise the circle for the eye. Turn piece over and press in the center of eye from behind to raise it. Repeat this technique on other lines of the design.

When complete, brush or rub on dark brown stain. Allow to set 15 minutes, rub off gently. When quite dry, rub hard with a soft cloth until the copper highlights glow and the grooves and dents are stained dark brown.

To make into a pendant, cut a piece of fairly heavy leather to the size shown (Fig. 2). Round corners. Punch holes as shown. If leather is light color, stain a deep brown. Liquid shoe polish is fine if you don't have leather stain. Or leather could be painted a color of your choice using diluted acrylic paint.

Fig. 1

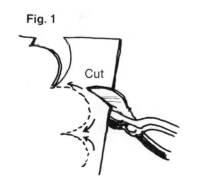

Cut

Fig. 2

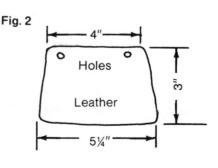

4"

Holes

Leather

3"

5¼"

53

EARRINGS

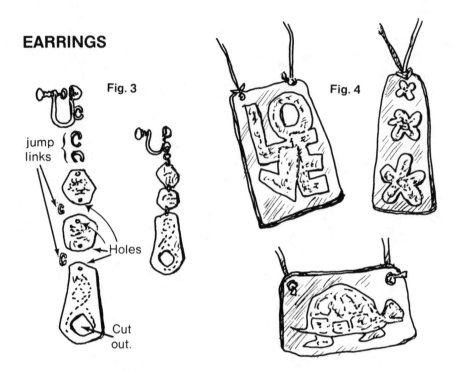

Fig. 3

jump links

Holes

Cut out.

Fig. 4

To attach copper to leather, use a fairly thick white or fabric glue. Position the copper bird on the leather and glue in place. Weight down while glue dries but be careful not to squash your embossing. Tie a thong to each corner of the leather piece to complete.

Earrings: It's easy to make earrings to go with the pendant from left-over scraps of copper. Cut three free-form shapes such as the ones shown in Fig. 3. If you'd like to make a cut out shape, use a small chisel. Place the copper on an old piece of wood. Hold chisel straight and hit with the hammer as many times as necessary to cut through the copper. Emboss the shapes as desired and finish as before. With an awl, punch holes at the top and bottom of middle pieces, and the top of last piece. Assemble with copper jump rings and attach to copper earring.

Now that you know the technique of working with copper, making copper jewelry of your own design should be easy. Draw paper patterns, adapting motifs with meanings for you—abstract shapes, flowers, etc. (Fig. 4).

Linked Copper Shapes

Earrings
(Iroquois)

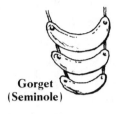

Gorget
(Seminole)

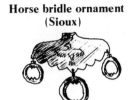

Horse bridle ornament
(Sioux)

Pendant
(Navaho)

Metal ornaments made by the Indians incorporate a number of traditional motifs. Above are silver ornaments from several areas. These forms, with linked shapes, were the inspirations for the copper jewelry creations in the next project. For these, you'll take pre-cut pieces of copper and beat them to give a hand-crafted look.

MATERIALS

Copper shapes; copper toilet lift wires (usually sold in pairs—one long, one short—with loops on top of each); fine copper wire; macramé beads with large holes (or shells or tumbled stones or other trims); copper jump links; clasp (if needed); leather thongs; epoxy glue; hammer; file or sandpaper; felt marker; narrow-nosed pliers; cutting pliers; awl.

Optional: drill, vise, anvil, copper pot cleaner, clear plastic spray.

Heavy-gauge copper shapes, made for copper enameling, are available in most craft stores and in catalogs of craft supplies. They come in a variety of precut shapes, some with holes for hanging. The jewelry creation you make will depend on the copper shapes you find available and how you assemble them. Below are general instructions for handling the copper, followed by specific ideas for various jewelry.

To remove the machine-made appearance and to achieve a rough, beaten look, lay the copper piece on a firm surface and beat it with a hammer. An anvil is the most practical surface for this purpose but if you don't have one, any small flat piece of heavy iron will do. You can even use a flat rock or concrete surface to pound onto. This will give an even rougher surface to the copper that is most effective. Pound the copper just enough to destroy the machine-made look.

Plan your jewelry, using as many pieces of copper as desired. Arrange the copper shapes on a table, together with any other units you are using—such as copper rods, pearls, beads, feathers, leather strips.

You can make holes in any shape to link pieces together. Mark the places for the holes with a felt marker. Hammer an awl tip into the copper. With a hand (or electric) drill, complete the holes.

File and sand all the edges and around the holes to make sure there are no rough places to catch on clothing.

You can make your own copper polish of equal parts of flour, salt and vinegar. One tablespoon of each will give you an adequate amount. Or you can polish the copper with copper pot cleaner. When each piece is finished (before adding trims), the copper can be sprayed with a clear finish to preserve the shine. Or the copper can be allowed to darken naturally, whichever is preferred.

Heavy copper wire (rods) can add distinction to some designs, such as the crescent pendant and chest piece. Copper replacement rods (toilet lift wires) are available in hardware stores. Hold the rod by the loop at the top and pound on each side. This will give a roughly square appearance to the rod. Pound the loop also.

To assemble jewelry, attach the pieces to each other with copper jump links. With narrow-nosed pliers, open a link, put it through the hole in the copper shape and close. Repeat the process on the other shape. Open a third link and insert it between the two links you've previously attached (Fig. 1). Or copper wire can be wound through open shapes to make loops for hanging (Fig. 2). Attach a link in the center wire. For some open shapes tie a thong directly through the hole (Fig. 3).

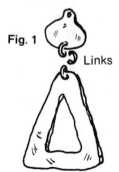

Fig. 1   Links

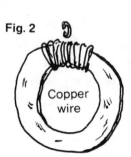

Fig. 2   Copper wire

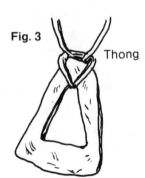

Fig. 3   Thong

Add trims. A contrasting beaten copper piece can be glued to form a double layer (Fig 4). Baroque stones or the smooth irregular shapes that are produced by a rock tumbler, complement the roughened copper. Blue and green stones or beads are good accent colors.

Trims should be attached with epoxy glue. After mixing the glue, use a toothpick to apply a tiny dab to the back of small stones or other added units. Do not use too much or it will show.

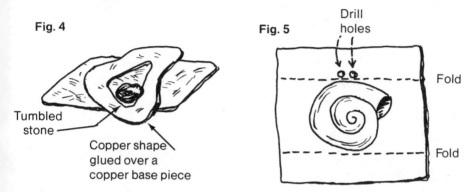

Fig. 4

Tumbled stone

Copper shape glued over a copper base piece

Fig. 5

Drill holes

Fold

Fold

That is the general procedure using standard copper shapes; here are a few specific suggestions.

A "Captured Treasure" pendant displays a small object you particularly treasure. Select a rectangular piece of copper in a size to suit the unit you wish to feature. The copper is folded to hold an exquisite stone, a gem piece (such as agate), coral or any special natural specimen. The one shown holds an iridescent spiral shell (**Fig. 5**).

Lay the shell on the copper to determine the size needed. Mark the fold lines with a felt marker.

On the top line, mark off the spots for two holes, near the center, to attach a hanging loop (Fig. 5). Make the holes.

To fold the copper, place the beaten piece in a vise and pound it, folding it at right angles on the lines marked, top and bottom (Fig. 6). Check the shell (or whatever you are using) to make sure it fits fairly snugly.

To make a hanging loop use fine copper wire and twist the ends inside (Fig. 7). Mix epoxy glue, and put a dab on the inside wire twist to secure it. Then glue the shell, or stone or whatever in position. When the glue is dry, hang the piece on thong or a cord (Fig. 8).

57

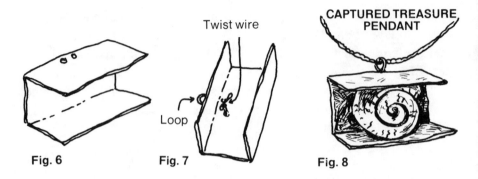

Twist wire

Loop

CAPTURED TREASURE PENDANT

Fig. 6   Fig. 7   Fig. 8

Crescent Pendant: Cut a piece of copper rod (lift wire) about 2½″ below the loop, using a wire cutter. Pound the rod closing the top loop slightly. Attach the rod to a crescent shaped piece of copper with epoxy glue. Allow to dry.

To attach the crescent more securely to the rod, use a piece of fine copper wire and wind in a figure eight in front and behind the crescent (Fig. 9). Add an extra turn around the bottom of the rod and slip on a link for a dangle. Secure the top and bottom wires with a dab of glue.

To make a dangle, cut a small piece of fine copper wire. Bend a small loop on one end, and insert the straight end into a bead. Form a hanging loop on the other end of the wire (Fig. 10). Slip the tip of a tiny feather up into the end of the bead, glue to hold.

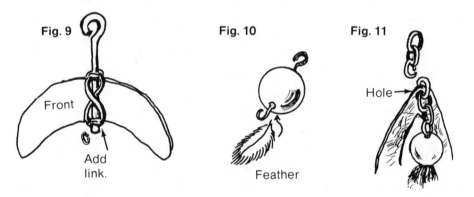

Fig. 9

Front

Add link.

Fig. 10

Feather

Fig. 11

Hole→

58

Slip a jump link in the hole of a dangle shape (Fig. 11), then add three more links above this one. Slip a jump link through the loop on top of the bead, add another link and slip this through the link attached to the top of the beaten copper shape. Link the dangle to the crescent (Fig. 12). Hang the pendant on a heavy thong.

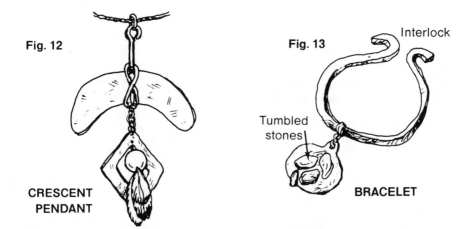

Fig. 12

Fig. 13

Interlock

Tumbled stones

CRESCENT PENDANT

BRACELET

Bracelet: With pliers, bend a loop in the straight end of the long lift wire (rod). Gently curve rod around into a bracelet shape (Fig. 13). Pound the wire to give it character. Try on and adjust the angles of the loops so they can interlock. With jump links or copper wire, attach as many decorated beaten copper dangles as you wish.

Chest Piece: Beads are strung on a thong that ties around the neck, coppers hang by links and rods (Fig. 15, see next page). Use the beads with large holes sold for macramé.

To get the spacing of the copper pieces and to determine the length needed for the wire rods, select copper pieces and pound them. Lay them out in the pattern they will form when assembled (Fig. 14).

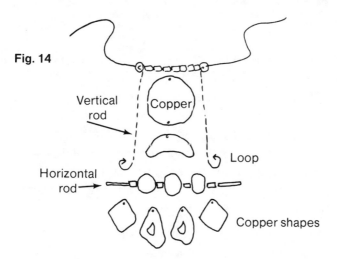

Fig. 14

Vertical rod

Copper

Loop

Horizontal rod

Copper shapes

59

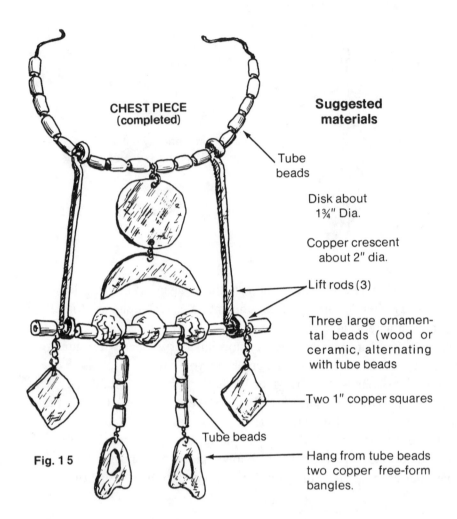

CHEST PIECE
(completed)

Suggested materials

Tube beads

Disk about 1¾″ Dia.

Copper crescent about 2″ dia.

Lift rods (3)

Three large ornamental beads (wood or ceramic, alternating with tube beads

Two 1″ copper squares

Tube beads

Hang from tube beads two copper free-form bangles.

Fig. 15

Cut a piece of thong about 22″ long (12″ plus enough on each end to tie). Slide a sufficient number of beads on the thong to allow room for the center copper units between the vertical rods.

You'll need two packages of lift wires for the rods. Measure the length for the vertical rods and add 1″ for a loop at the bottom. Mark and cut off. Bend the tips into loops to accommodate the horizontal wire, making sure that the loops are at proper angles to the top loops. Slide the top loop of one of the rods onto the thong, add necessary number of beads, and slide the top loop of the second rod onto the thong.

To determine the length of the horizontal rod, slide on the beads and end loops of the vertical rods, add a bead at each end. Mark the length of the rod, slide off the beads and cut the rod.

Drill all the holes necessary, pound the copper rods. Sand the edges and ends.

For the hanging units at the bottom, slide three beads (or as many as desired) onto a piece of fine copper wire. Make small loops at the top and bottom of the wire, and push the ends of wire back into beads (Fig. 16). Add two jump links at the top. Link on a beaten copper unit at bottom. Repeat for a second unit. Add four or five links to the top of each of two beaten copper squares.

Assemble the horizontal rod (Fig. 17). Slide the rod through the links above the square piece, through the loop of the horizontal rod, through the beads, through the top loop of the beaded hanging unit, through more beads, etc., until all are in place. Add beads at each end of the rod and glue them in place. The chest piece is complete.

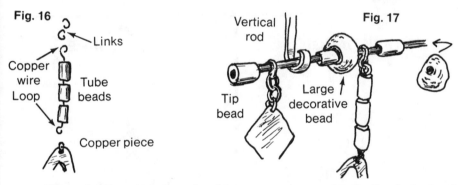

Fig. 16

Links

Copper wire

Loop

Tube beads

Copper piece

Vertical rod

Fig. 17

Tip bead

Large decorative bead

These body ornaments should start your own ideas. Look in hardware and plumbing supply stores. There are all sorts of shapes made of pure copper to adapt to jewelry. The trick is to see them out of context, beaten, and combined with beads or trims. When you can do this, you are well started on creative jewelry. Other ideas for linked, beaten copper jewelry are shown below and on the next page.

TIE PIN OR BROOCHES

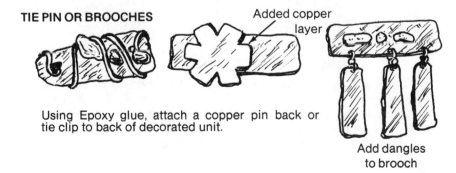

Added copper layer

Using Epoxy glue, attach a copper pin back or tie clip to back of decorated unit.

Add dangles to brooch

61

NECKLACE

Tumbled
stones

Bead a necklace of bulky beads, suspend copper shapes by links.

CHOKER

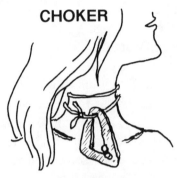

Slip thong through existing hole in copper, wind thong twice around neck, tie in front.

DISK DANGLE

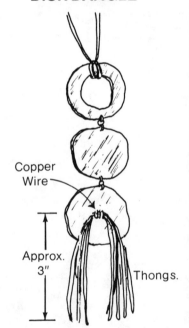

Copper
Wire

Approx.
3"

Thongs.

Suspend three circular shapes. Wind center of thin strips of thong (or decorative cord) with copper wire. Glue onto last disk.

HANGING
BEAD LAVALIERE

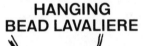

Beads

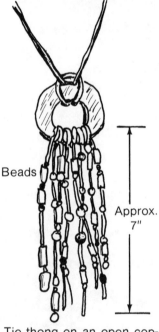

Approx.
7"

Tie thong on an open copper circle. Tie cords or thongs below. String, knot, or glue on beads at various levels.

ᴮBone Jewelry

The Indians utilized the bones of the animals they hunted for practical or decorative purposes. Horns and antlers were also made into weapons, tools and figurines, among other uses. Large bones and ivory were used for tools, some were carved or etched to make decorative objects. Teeth, claws and tiny whole bones were used for ornamenting garments and making necklaces.

Working with bone requires patience but the results can often be lovely, almost like a piece of ivory. Bones vary considerably. Chicken bones are brittle and do not polish well. Beef bones are sturdy but vary in color according to the part used. Bones from a leg of lamb or ham could also be used. You'll have to experiment to see which bone works best and creates the color and texture needed for what you are making.

Some craft dealers carry processed bones for jewelry making.

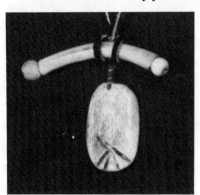

MATERIALS

Bones; jewelry findings; a few beads; thong; powdered pumice (optional); vise; hacksaw; coping or jewelry saw; files; awl; rough and fine sandpaper; black or umber acrylic paint; hand drill; baking soda.

Select bones available and plan what to make.

To prepare the bones, clean them thoroughly. Place the bone in the vise. With a hacksaw, cut off unusable ends of the bone (Fig. 1). If a circular piece is planned, cut some crosswise pieces. For flat bone pieces, cut bone vertically (Fig. 2). Clean the bone and remove the marrow.

To "cure" add about a tablespoon of baking soda to a pan of water and boil the bone pieces for about an hour. Rinse thoroughly. Place outside in the sun for several days to bleach and dry. Give the bones plenty of time to dry and harden before working.

63

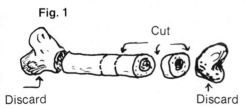

Fig. 1

Cut

Discard

Discard

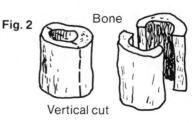

Fig. 2

Bone

Vertical cut

Plan the designs you want to cut. Draw sketches of units to suit the shape of the bones you have. See Figures 4, 7, 10, 12, 13, 14, 15 for ideas. Draw the design on the bone.

Use the vise to hold the bone piece while cutting. Pad the jaws of the vise with a soft cloth. Place bone in the vise but not too tightly. Although bone is very hard it will crack. You must learn to judge how tight to make the vise.

Cut out the shapes desired, using the coping saw. When cutting cross shapes (Fig. 8, 11), keep turning the bone piece. The angle of the bone is often misleading. By turning, you'll know if you are cutting properly all around.

To finish surface, begin by using coarse metal files. Use a flat file for the outside of the piece, round files to get to inner curves of the bone. Use a file brush to keep files clean as you work. File out any remaining marrow and porous bone. File down to hard ivory-like bone. Continue shaping piece as you file. With a finer-toothed file, perfect the shape, round the edges, and smooth the surface.

For decorations, the edge of the file can be used to make indentations along edges (Fig. 3). To engrave a motif, scratch it onto the surface with a knife or awl. Small dots can be made by using the drill (Fig. 4), but drill into surface only slightly.

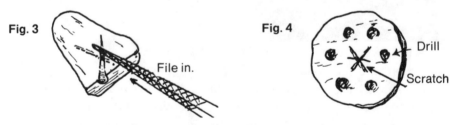

Fig. 3   File in.

Fig. 4   Drill   Scratch

To bring out designs, fill scratched areas with a little black or umber acrylic paint. When dry, sand to remove paint on surface.

Drill holes where needed in order to add jump rings to make into the jewelry planned.

Continue smoothing, first with the rough then fine sandpaper. Sand with the grain of the bone, not across. After using the finest grade of sandpaper, if a smoother surface is desired, finish with powdered pumice. Make a paste of a little pumice and water, and rub it vigorously on the bone. Polish with a soft cloth. This gives a lovely patina.

Below are a few suggested shapes to make of bone with ideas for making them into jewelry. Some bones have such interesting shapes that they can be utilized just as they are. Once you become adept and get the feel of the difference in bones, you can cut curves or make openwork

Pendant: Remove marrow of a 3″ length of bone with an awl and a small round file (Fig. 5). Using epoxy glue, glue a bead about ¼″ in diameter to each end of the long bone. Cut a thong 24″ long—tie to long bone (Fig. 6). Prepare a flat piece of (beef) bone about 1″ x 1½″. Drill a hole at the top. Tie a piece of nylon fishing line through hole of flat piece, then thread the line up through a bead, and tie to the middle of the long bone (Fig. 7). Add a dab of glue to secure. Trim ends.

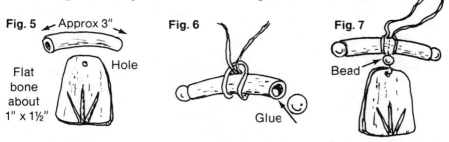

Fig. 5 ⟵ Approx 3″ ⟶

Flat
bone
about
1″ x 1½″

Hole

Fig. 6

Glue

Fig. 7

Bead

Necklace: String colorful beads or wooden beads interspersed with bone pieces in which you have drilled holes (Fig. 8). Make an ornament to hang from the necklace by suspending a bead inside a bone ring. Bring wire or thread up through the hole in the bone, through a bead and attach to necklace (Fig. 9). Make three of these hanging units, or as many as desired (Fig. 10).

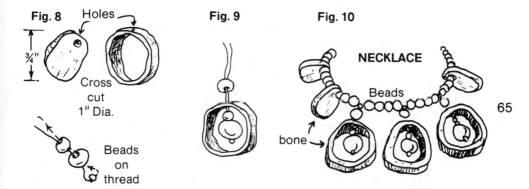

Fig. 8   Holes

¾″

Cross
cut
1″ Dia.

Beads
on
thread

Fig. 9

Fig. 10

NECKLACE

Beads

bone ⟶

65

 **Fig. 11**

Fig. 12

RING

Ring: Find a bone piece that should be about the proper size for a ring once the marrow and the porous bone next to the marrow are filed out (Fig. 11). Mark and cut the ring. Shape with a file. File inside thoroughly with round file. Sand and polish. Engrave a design on the top (Fig. 12), or glue on a stone using epoxy glue.

Fig. 13   **EARRINGS**   **Fig. 14**

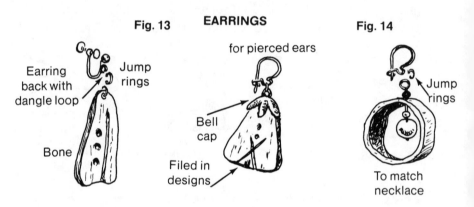

Earrings: Cut the bone shape desired. Drill a hole at the top. Using jump links, attach the shape to earring findings of the type desired (Fig. 13). Or instead of drilling a hole, attach bell cap at top. Make earrings to match necklace or pendant (Fig. 14).

TIE CLIP

Fig. 15

Tie pin: Shape a bone piece (Fig. 15) to fit on a tie pin backing (available in craft supply stores). Attach to back with epoxy glue.

66

The possibilities of bone are determined only by your imagination. Make bone and bead, or bone and shell neckpieces. Combine bone and feathers: Drill a hole in a piece of bone, insert glue and add feathers. Natural elements combine well when organized and planned.

Neckbone Necklace

Many fascinating shapes occur in nature, but it takes imagination to see their potential. The contour of neck bones of chicken or turkey and the proverbial wishbone can be made into jewelry that is sure to stir comments.

If you are lucky enough to find bones that have been cleaned and bleached by nature, they are even better. The neck bones of a bird or the spine of a snake are exotic and easily strung because the holes are built in. Should you find such bones, use as is, white and sun-bleached.

MATERIALS: Neckbones; beads; wishbone; nylon stringing line; necklace catch; spray paint.

Clean bones well and cure as before, bleaching in the sun. If you are using chicken bones, they may not bleach white. When the bone color is irregular, it's better to paint or stain them. When bones are thoroughly dry and clean, spray paint color desired.

String bones, alternating with complementary colored beads. (Fig. 1). To add a wishbone, drill hole in the flat top of the bone, and string on. Continue stringing the other side. When you reach the proper length, tie on a catch at back. Secure with a dab of glue. Trim ends.

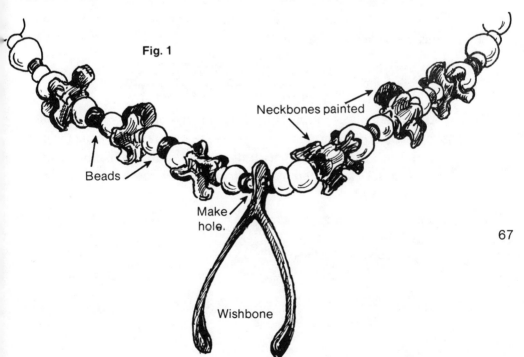

Fig. 1

Neckbones painted

Beads

Make hole.

Wishbone

67

Leather and Bone Pectoral

Pectorals or ornaments worn on the chest, were made by Western and Plains Indians. Originally, they may have been used for protection, later they were worn for ceremonial purposes.

This one uses leather strips for holding the elements together—another practical Indian idea. It is a jewelry fashion that can be quite dramatic. Bamboo, tube beads, handmade beads, hair pipe beads, etc., could be substituted for the bone.

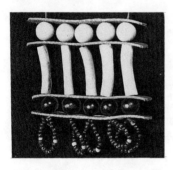

MATERIALS

A piece of fairly heavy leather, enough for four strips ½" x 4¼"; ten wooden beads; five pieces of bone ⅜" in diameter, or purchased bone tube beads 2" long; narrow thong or cord about 36" long; seed or "real" beads; leather punch or awl.

Chicken wing bones can be used but other bones about ⅜" diameter are more sturdy. Cut bones about 1¾" long. Clean out marrow, cure and sand surface smooth.

Cut the four leather strips, round the corners. Punch five holes, evenly space across (Fig. 1).

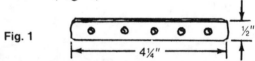

Fig. 1

½"

4¼"

Assemble units as shown (Fig. 2). Knot end of cord. Go up through hole in left of bottom leather piece (Fig. 3), through bead, through next leather hole, through bone, leather, bead, leather. Then go over to the second hole in the top leather strip and start down next row until unit is assembled.

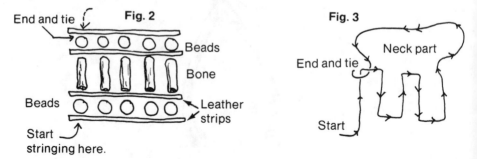

68

Fig. 2

End and tie

Beads

Bone

Beads

Leather strips

Start stringing here.

Fig. 3

Neck part

End and tie

Start

Make a knot close against top of leather strip. For neckpiece, allow about 24″ of cord or thong to fit over head. Then make a knot to go above left side of leather piece and then go back down, in through top left hole. Tie above bead. Add a little glue to tie. Cut off and push ends down into the bead.

If desired, add a fringe of small beads on the bottom (Fig. 4). String beads on thread and tie onto thong where it comes through the holes in bottom of leather piece.

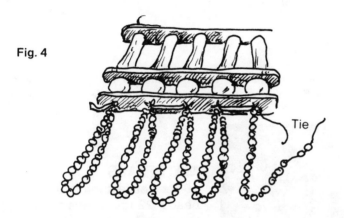

Fig. 4

Tie

If you don't want to work with bone, substitute three barrel or six pony or tile beads for each bone in center section.

Leather strips can also be hung vertically with thong passing through ends of strips (Fig. 5).

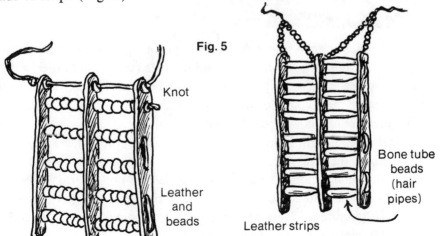

Fig. 5

Knot

Leather and beads

Leather strips

Bone tube beads (hair pipes)

Jewelry of Mixed Materials

Indian adornments were often an effective combination of leather and other small elements such as feathers, pebbles, fur tails, seeds, animal claws, hoofs, teeth, etc. A feather necklace can be an exciting and original accent for your wardrobe.

In making your own feather necklaces, you can use poultry feathers, feathers from game birds, or purchased feathers. Most craft supply places have feathers of several types, available in many colors.

Feather and Thong

This feathered necklace has the dignified, mellow look of fine jewelry. It can easily be more flamboyant, however — just use brighter colors and bigger feathers.

MATERIALS

16 feet of leather thong; 2 barrel beads, 22 round wooden beads, 7 large oval wooden beads (natural or brown); 2 packages of tippet feathers about 2" long; white or fabric glue; clip clothespins.

Tippet feathers can be purchased in a sporting goods store that carries supplies for those who tie their own fishing flies (or by mail order, see p. 221). Golden pheasant tippets and plain pheasant tippets were chosen here because the colors blended so well with natural wooden beads, but other feathers and colors could be effective also.

Choose beads with large holes such as those sold for macramé.

To make the necklace, cut four strips of thong about 4 feet long each. The thong should be about ⅛" wide and not too thick. Plastic lacing is similar and could be used. Take three strips and start braiding about 10" from end. Hold end with clip clothespin. Braid about 3½", hold with another clip clothespin (Fig. 1).

70

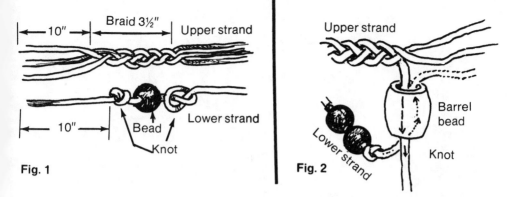

Fig. 1

Fig. 2

For second (lower) strand, use **fourth** piece of thong. Tie a knot about 10″ from end. Slide thong through a round bead, up to knot, tie another knot below bead (Fig. 1). Push on another bead, tie a knot and repeat until you have strung on five beads, ending with a knot.

Oval beads will be set vertically between two strands. Lay the braided piece in position, beaded strand below. Slide one strand of the braid *down* through the oval bead as shown (Fig. 2). Slide end of beaded strand *up* through oval bead. Push oval bead up against end of braid. The third strand of the braid now becomes a bead strand. Bead strand now gets braided.

Continue braiding, about 1″ more and hold with clothespin. On lower (bead) strand, tie a knot as it comes out of the vertical or oval bead, holding vertical bead in position. Add a round bead, knot, add another round bead and knot.

Then push lower (bead) strand up through another oval bead. Bring one strand of the braid down through the oval bead as before (Fig. 3). Repeat this process until you have the seven oval (vertical) beads in place. For end, braid the 3½″ to match the other side and add the five beads on lower strand, knotting between them.

To finish ends and make a tie for the necklace, gather the four strands on one side and push into a barrel bead. Cut one of the braided strands short so the end of it will disappear into the barrel bead. Put glue on this strand and slide the barrel bead up over the cut end, and against the last knot and braid (Fig. 3). Repeat on other side.

71

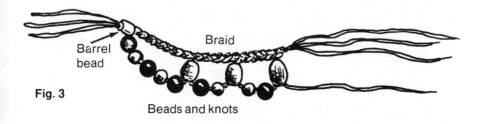

Fig. 3

Beads and knots

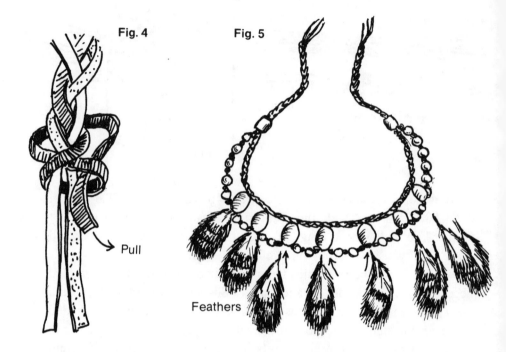

Fig. 4   Fig. 5

Pull

Feathers

When the glue is dry, braid the remaining three strips for ties. When nearly to the end, wrap one end twice around the other two, slip this end down inside the wrapped part and pull to knot (Fig. 4).

A sturdy, pretty necklace is now complete, but the addition of feathers makes it unique.

To add feathers, put the necklace on a flat surface, shaping it to a somewhat circular position as it will fit around the neck. Lay out the feathers you plan to use (Fig. 5). Arrange them, planning enough for each oval (vertical) bead and noting general shape. Some feathers curve to the right, others to left depending on which side of the bird they came from. Place larger feathers towards center, the shape of the feathers on each side should match as much as possible. If feathers are small, plan several for each bead.

When feathers make a pleasing arrangement, they are ready to be inserted. With a toothpick, tuck some glue in between the cords, inside one of the oval beads. Gently, without disturbing the delicate shape of the feather, push the quill end into the bead. Repeat, inserting feathers into each of the vertical beads. Test necklace to be sure feathers lie properly when worn. Allow glue to dry. Necklace is complete.

72

Variations: This beading method is simple and easily adaptable to cords, yarn, string or other macramé materials. More feathers can be accommodated if you use more vertical beads and space them closer together. The vertical beads, necessary for holding feathers, can be handmade beads, tubular type or barrel.

Most craft supply places carry feathers for making feather flowers. These come in a great variety of color and sizes, that can make fluffy, wildly-colored neck adornments. Most catalogs show shapes of turkey or goose feathers. The size should be about 3″-4″ long. Exotic effects can be achieved with plumes, ostrich or peacock feathers.

If you have some interesting beads with small holes from an old necklace, that you'd like to combine with vertical beads with large holes, you can use the same technique with two beading threads to make top and bottom rows. Solidly bead top and bottom strands (Fig. 6), using nylon line. Go through vertical beads both ways, as before, to position the large-holed beads. It will be necessary to experiment as to how many beads are needed between verticals, on top and the bottom strand, so necklace will lie flat around the neck. The number depends on size and shape of in-between beads. After stringing, add appropriate feathers. Make them fluffy and big, or neat and small. Maybe a pet parakeet has shed enough feathers for this purpose. For the closing sew on a regular jewelry clasp.

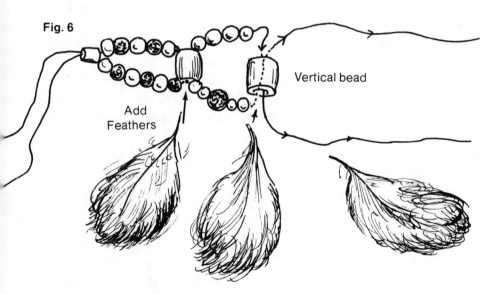

Fig. 6

Add Feathers

Vertical bead

73

Bead and Seed Necklace

The Indians used seeds for ornaments or decorations long before they used beads. In ancient times seeds were strung with claws or other materials to make necklaces. When seeds were used for decoration they were either attached to each other or sewn on a background.

A necklace of seeds and beads requires patience, but the elegant result is well worth the effort.

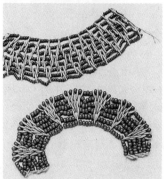

MATERIALS
Seeds (cantalope or honeydew); beads of one color (seed or "real"); jewelry clasp; beading or regular needle; nylon or other strong thread.

Prepare seeds by washing thoroughly, then placing in a pan in a "low" oven until they are completely dried. If you plan to use "real" beads, a regular needle will fit through beads for stringing and it is strong enough to pierce the seeds. However, if using seed beads, you'll need a beading needle which is *not* strong enough to pierce the seeds. Then it's necessary to prepare the seeds beforehand by pushing holes in *each* end of *each* seed with a sturdy needle.

Basic stringing technique: You will string on row after row of beads, seeds, beads; each row getting increasingly larger (Fig. 1).

To start, tie a bead on the end of a thread, go through one end of a seed, string on the proper number of beads, more seeds, repeating all across row. Try around neck to determine size needed for top row. Each

Start stringing here.

Fig. 1

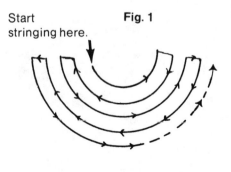

Fig. 2

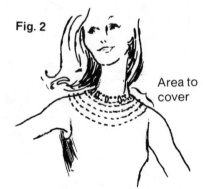

Area to cover

succeeding row should be larger to cover neck and shoulder area (Fig. 2). Finished unit should lie flat and smooth.

Below are two different patterns that can be created by placement of beads and seeds (Fig. 3). You will need to adjust them to your materials. Variations in seed or bead sizes can greatly affect how the necklace lies. Check its contours frequently as you work to make sure that it doesn't flare out too much or isn't so straight it won't lie properly across your shoulders.

Fig. 3

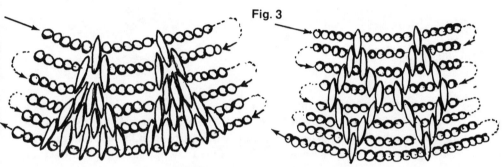

Only two repeats are shown; repeat as many times as needed.

At end of each row, finish off with a seed (Fig. 4). After the last seed, string on a bead. Go back through the top hole in the seed, back out at the lower end, add a bead, thread back through lower hole of this seed. String through top of new seed for lower row. Now you are ready to start stringing (and counting) units for next row.

In working the pattern, go through the top of seeds on the row you are doing, then on the next row below go through the bottom of those seeds, as well as the tops of seeds for the row you are now working on.

When complete, tie a cord at the back top corners for tying on, or sew on a regular jewelry clasp.

All sorts of seeds can be used. Experiment to find what effects can be achieved.

Fig. 4

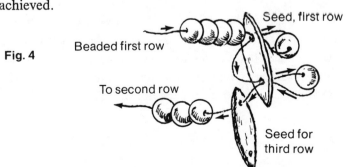

Seed, first row

Beaded first row

To second row

Seed for third row

Earrings: Bead-Dangles

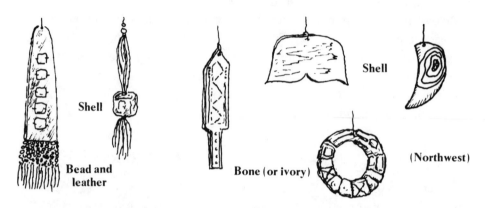

Shell

Shell

(Northwest)

Shell

Bead and leather

Bone (or ivory)

There are not many examples of earrings from any of the Indian cultures. Some tribes probably slipped bone or other natural materials through a slit in the ear lobe. Others probably wore ornaments of shell, bone or metal. The earrings sketched above were exhibited in the case of a museum hall devoted to Northwest Indian crafts, and can provide ideas for earrings of your own.

Little needs altering to adapt the earrings sketched so that they have a "now" look.

MATERIALS
Pair of earring backs (type desired) with loops to attach drops; scrap leather about ⅛" thick; fine nylon fishing line; awl; "real" beads; fine yarn (or embroidery floss); yarn and regular needles; needle threader; tumbled shell pieces (optional).

For pattern, trace shape shown in Fig. 1. Draw two pattern outlines on a piece of leather. Any small scraps will do such as: leather trim from other projects, trim off a belt that was too long, a section from a discarded bag or wallet. Leather is very durable and reusable. For earrings, it should be firmer than chamois but not too thick.

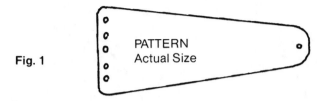

Fig. 1

PATTERN
Actual Size

Cut out shapes with a sharp knife or single-edge razor blade. If color of cut edges looks too raw, use a little liquid shoe polish to darken.

For beading holes, use an awl or heavy needle to punch five holes at the bottom of each leather shape. Using a medium needle, thread on a 3″ piece of yarn that is as thick as possible but will still go through the beads. A needle threader is helpful here. You may have to split some yarn to get proper thickness.

To attach beads, bring needle up from back, then down through the same hole, leaving a loop above (Fig. 2). Bring loose end, and the end threaded on the needle, both up through loop as shown (Fig. 3) leaving both ends long enough for beading. Pull loop tight. String six or seven beads on one of the two ends, tie knot at end. Leave 1″ of yarn below beads, and trim off. Thread other loose end on needle. String on six or seven beads (Fig. 4), knot, trim to 1″. Repeat in other five holes.

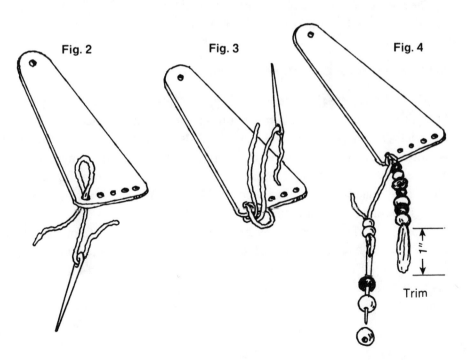

Fig. 2

Fig. 3

Fig. 4

1″

Trim

77

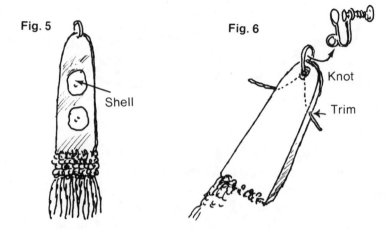

Fig. 5

Shell

Fig. 6

Knot

Trim

The leather can be left plain or tiny shell-like buttons can be sewn or glued on. Some craft suppliers carry irregularly-shaped shell fragments or tumbled stones. These are very attractive glued to the leather (Fig. 5). Use epoxy glue.

To attach leather piece to earring, thread fine nylon fishing line on needle, and sew a hanging loop at top of leather. Knot and sew back inside leather thickness to hide the ends (Fig. 6). Trim off excess. Slip this loop on earring loop. Or use a jump ring to attach dangle to earring loop. Repeat for other earring.

The choice of color is yours, but simple colors are most effective, and more reminiscent of the original inspiration.

Other Beaded Earrings

Assorted beads: In this example (Fig. 7), beads are strung on yarn. Use yarn as thick as possible to go through beads used. Beads should be a variety of shapes and sizes, pony beads, homemade, shell pieces, wooden beads, etc. in whatever combinations you like. Bead one-half of a piece of yarn. Tie middle to earring loop and continue beading down other side. Beads should hang down 2½" to 3" from earring. Thin thongs could be used in a similiar manner.

Leave 1" tufts of yarn below beads, trim. If a larger tuft of yarn is desired at the end, cut several 1½" yarn pieces, tie around yarn used for stringing (Fig. 8). Pull last bead down below knot insert fabric glue inside it and put bead up over yarn ties to cover and hold. When dry, trim ends evenly, 1" long.

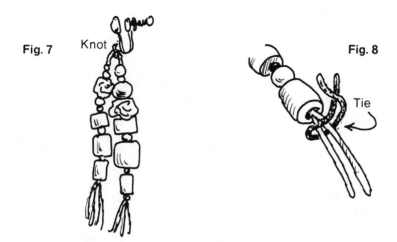

Fig. 7 Knot

Fig. 8 Tie

Special bead dangle: These examples (Fig. 9) feature a special object or decorative bead. Fold a 7″ yarn piece in half, tie middle to earring loop. Slip both strands through a bead, string each strand through separate beads. Put two strands through one bead and continue.

Hold up to ear to determine length you'd like. At end, put both strands through the special, large bead. Tie knot below. Instead of large bead, this could be a piece of etched bone or shell with hole, or a shaped and carved wooden piece. It's also a clever way to show off a pair of some meaningful, tiny objects.

Make a yarn tuft below, adding extra yarn if desired. Or add a feather, glue it and trim away extra yarn. All sorts of variations on this theme are possible.

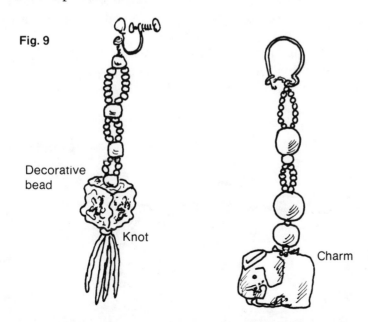

Fig. 9

Decorative bead

Knot

Charm

79

Ankle Wrap

Many Indian dances were accompanied by rattling or jingling sounds from ornaments attached to the dancer's knees, elbows or ankles. Bells are used now and are an outcome of trade with Europeans. Formerly, diverse materials such as small turtle shells, pieces of animal horn or hoofs were used for rattle sounds. Bell sounds came from the jingling of copper and silver beads. In some areas, metal was beaten thin and curved into a cone shape. When strung together, these made a bell-like sound. In the Northwest, Puffin beaks strung together, were the source of sounds during dances and rituals.

Here is a quick way to make a mod, jingly ankle wrap.

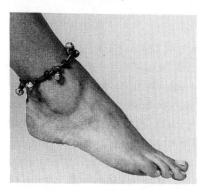

MATERIALS

Six ½" "Jingle" bells (or decorative bells); 22" piece of leather thong (about ³⁄₁₆" wide, ⅛" thick), or decorative cord; five pony beads.

To assemble, slide a bell onto the thong about 3" from the end. Tie a knot over the loop of the bell (Fig. 1). If the loop to bell is too small, knot the thong next to the bell.

Slide on a bead. Then slide on another bell and knot. (If knotting thong next to bell, do so on each side). Space bells about 1" apart. Continue around, alternating bells and beads.

To wear, tie the ends around ankle. Respace units if necessary for length desired. Make in other lengths to wear on your arm.

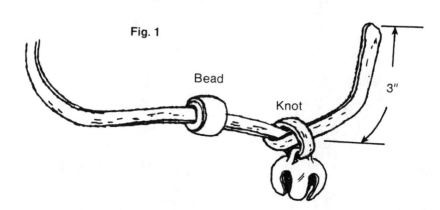

Fig. 1 Bead Knot 3"

CLOTHING

2

Pueblo
(Hopi)

Wrapped skirt
with cloak
(Northwest)

Apron, front
and back
(West Coast)

The Indians wore practical clothing suited to the climate they lived in. Style was based generally on the most efficient way to utilize the materials that were available. In very hot climates, a loin cloth or simple wrapped skirt was adequate. In cool climates, layers of clothing were added as needed.

Of all materials, leather was the most readily available to the Indians. Leather refers to any skin which has been tanned so that it will remain soft and pliable. Once a skin has been treated to keep it from spoiling, it is extremely durable.

The bear and buffalo hides were too heavy for most clothing purposes. Usually the best leather came from the deer (buckskin). Hides of small animals such as beaver, ermine and jackrabbit were used in some areas. The Eskimos used seal and walrus skin also.

How the leather is processed determines the type of surface created. Various parts of the hide had different uses. The heavier parts were used for knife cases, moccasin soles, thongs, etc. Thinner inner parts were more suited to garments, but often the entire skin was used. The aminal's contours sometimes were retained on the lower edges of the garment.

Basically, all garments were practical, serving as protection from the surrounding climate. But the Indian's sense of design was also apparent as the garments very often had some sort of ornamentation.

Most skirts were merely a piece of leather, wrapped around and tied at the waist and overlapped on the left thigh. The purpose was not fashion as we know it today, but pure practicality. When a woman was spinning or rolling fibers to make rope or cord, she rolled it against her thigh. Efficiency, therefore, dictated the design of her garment.

In temperate climates, the simple basic garment was a tube shape made by sewing the skins together. Setting in of sleeves and legs was unknown, except to the Eskimo who did excellent tailoring. Sometimes a yoke was created by adding a third skin or cloth between the first two skins. Separate sleeves were also worn, with ties front and back to hold in place. Leggings were tube-like covers for the legs and outer thigh but were not seamed to each other.

As the weather became increasingly cold and severe, the Indians used robes for warmth. These served to mitigate the discomforts of bitter weather. When moving about, a robe was used as a cloak or mantle. When sleeping, it became a blanket. Hides of many animals were made into blanket-robes: bear, elk and the familiar buffalo skin. Sometimes the fur was left on when processing the hide. In the Southwest, turkey feathers were spiraled around cords to make a fabric used for blankets. Other Indians used strips of rabbit skin.

Of course, clothing varied from tribe to tribe, each with its individual adaptation of materials available and suitable for its particular way of life. Most traditional clothing styles, up to the last century, were handed down from ancient times. A few of the old styles from different areas are sketched.

The Indians also created woven materials from various fibers and animal hairs, but we will discuss weaving techniques in the second part of this chapter.

(Plains)

Side slit
skirt
(Eastern)

With separate
tied-on sleeves
(North-East)

Sewing

Fabrics—sewing stitches: This is not a book on sewing; there is too much else to cover. Let's assume you have some acquaintance with sewing methods. With a few hints, tips and a lot of practice you can take off with your own inspirations. You *can* make it.

Choosing materials: The impact of whatever you make depends to a large extent on the careful selection of materials. Colors, textures, size of added units—such as beads and trims—all determine its success. Deep and light tones, soft suedes, shiny beads—consider all these aspects as you choose materials. You may pick a soft enticing fabric, be captivated by some intriguing pattern for a lining. But put them together along with the trim you plan to use to make certain they are effective. No one can really tell until they are juxtaposed.

Materials: There is a vast array of materials available today in all sorts of synthetic, as well as natural, fibers. Each has its own characteristics with which you should become familiar as you handle it. If a weave or fiber content is new to you, sew up some scrap pieces to get the feel and nature of it.

With velvet, corduroy and velour, be careful when pressing. Do not flatten the texture. For leather, see below.

Check the pattern you purchase, fitting it to your own measurements, making sure it is right size in all directions. Mark any variations and adjustments on the pattern. Cut and sew accurately, following instructions. Sewing great put-ons is a matter of taste and imagination in selection and care in making.

Working with leather: Only recently have we really begun to re-appreciate the beauty and quality of leather. It is only slightly more difficult to sew than fabric. If you have some skill in making your own clothes, be venturesome and make something in leather. Most stores selling leather have booklets with basic techniques on how to cut and sew the leather. They will help you select the proper leather needed. Patterns designed for leather also have instructions included. Be sure to use a pattern adaptable for leather. Try a simple garment first, such as a vest or bag. Take the pattern with you when selecting the hide.

Very briefly, remember these things when sewing leather:

LEATHER

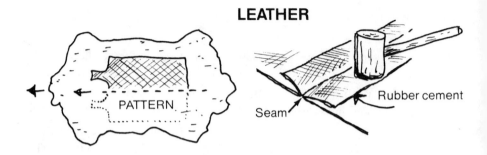

PATTERN

Seam

Rubber cement

Cutting: The pattern must follow the center line of the hide. This was the backbone of the animal and determines the grain of the leather. Put the neck of the pattern towards the neck of hide; the center back, center front, etc., parallel to the backbone line. If pattern calls for two of the same piece, cut only one thickness at a time and turn pattern over to cut other side. Pin only in seam allowance (never into body of leather), or tape pattern to leather. You may also trace pattern with a felt pen.

To Sew: Use long stitch on the machine. Check tension. It may need slight adjustment. Use a strong thread such as cotton-wrapped polyester. *Seams and Hems:* At ends of seams, do not back stitch. Leave threads hanging and then tie securely. Finish seam edges with seam binding or glue them open with rubber cement. Apply cement with a small brush, then pound seam open with a wooden mallet. If necessary, lift seam, adjust and lay seam flat again. Remove any excess cement with a small lump of dried rubber cement. Cement hems in place.

Always make garment long and large enough. Once sewn, leather garments cannot be let out.

Fakes: There are all kinds of fabulous fake leathers and pretend pelts, in textures of all kinds. Suede cloth is easier to handle than suede leather. Vinyl leather sews much like real leather and like leather should be sewn as little as possible. Any pinning or stitching will show. Seams of vinyl should also be glued open.

Fake furs handle like any very heavy fabric. Cut on the wrong side to be able to see what you are doing. Choose only very simple patterns, and make sure nap is all in the same direction.

Stitches for Hand Sewing: Several basic stitches will be mentioned for sewing on cloth. Below are diagrams of the stitches.

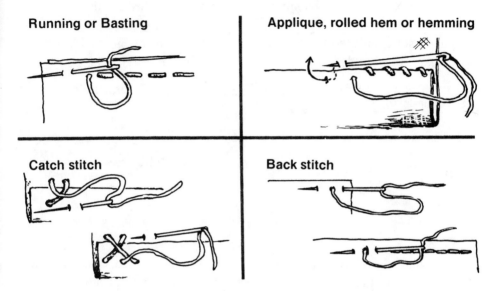

Running or Basting

Applique, rolled hem or hemming

Catch stitch

Back stitch

Fringes: To add a fringe of yarn or cord along on edge, follow this simple procedure. Cut fringe pieces twice desired length.
1. Pull loop up through fabric with small crochet hook.
2. Slip ends back through loop.
3. Pull tight.
4. Repeat at even intervals. Trim evenly.

Fringe

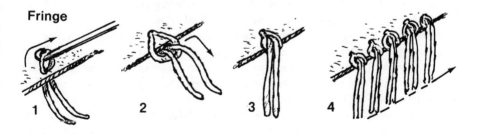

1   2   3   4

85

Drawstring: Occasionally you may have to insert a drawstring. This is how it is made: After fabric is sewn up, fold the hem down to make a channel. There should be an opening at each side, but you can cut slits if necessary (Fig. 1).

Cut drawstring cord twice length needed to allow pull cords on both sides. To aid in threading cord through channel, attach safety pin on one end of cord, thread completely around, inside the channel. Then go through channel a second time, but when reaching the slit on the opposite side, slide cord out and leave a loop of the necessary length hanging out for drawstring loop on that side (Fig. 2). Then go back

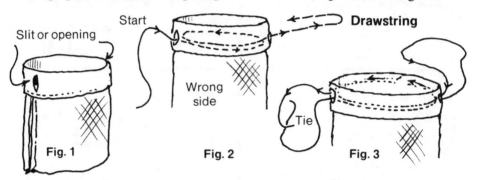

into channel and complete going around for the second time. Tie end to first end of the cord (Fig. 3), creating loop hanging out that side. Turn piece right side out. Pull on the loops on each side to close.

Other sewing methods and ideas will be described on each project.

Garments

Vest Ideas

There is little evidence that the early Indians wore vests. However, a vest offers all sorts of possibilities for Indian-inspired trim.

If you have a favorite vest that fits well, use it for a pattern to make a new one. Lay the vest flat on a large piece of paper. Draw all around back, along edges. Turn and, on another piece of paper, draw around one front side. Add exact seam allowance. Allow for darts and hem. Remove vest. Cut out the paper pattern. Pin paper pieces together to make sure you've reproduced its shape exactly. Try the pattern on to get an idea of the fit. Then use the paper pattern to cut a vest of new fabric. If you are doubtful of the fit, make the pattern up quickly in scrap fabric, machine basting the seams. Or buy a pattern. There will be instructions on how to make it up.

The choice of fabric is yours. Try leather and cut in some fringes, or choose a velure that feels soft and rich. Add fringes made of chamois or yarn.

Here is a "for instance" with suggested trim to try:

MATERIALS

Vest pattern, long and straight; 1½ yards tan velour; 1½ yards lining material (or amount suggested on pattern—lining material should be lightweight cotton or gay print such as orange and brown); pair of brown suede leather elbow patches; assortment of wooden and other medium large beads (brown, orange, etc); 1 yard leather thong; fabric glue.

Pin pattern on fabric, neck end of each piece facing same end of fabric. Color will be affected if pieces go in different directions. Follow instruction on pattern for fabric with "nap."

Cut out. Cut pieces for lining. Sew up darts (if any). Sew side and shoulder seams. Carefully steam open velure seams. Sew darts, side and shoulder seams on lining.

Pin lining inside vest, matching seams and edges.

Turn vest edges inside ½", turn lining edges under ¾" and pin all around. Thus ¼" of velure shows along inside edge (Fig. 1) of vest. Hand sew lining to vest at all edges except hem.

At bottom, turn up hem. Catch-stitch. Turn lining hem inside, pinning it ¾" shorter than edge of velure of vest (Fig. 2). Hem lining separately.

Fig. 1

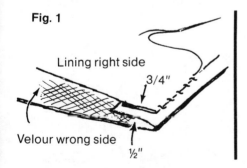

Lining right side

3/4"

Velour wrong side

½"

Fig. 2

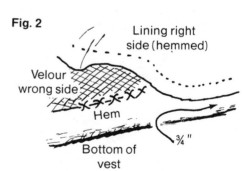

Lining right side (hemmed)

Velour wrong side

Hem

¾"

Bottom of vest

87

Vest is now complete and ready to decorate. Around the bottom of the vest add a leather fringe or a fur edging. Some stores carry these by the yard. Or work in a yarn type fringe (see page 85), if desired.

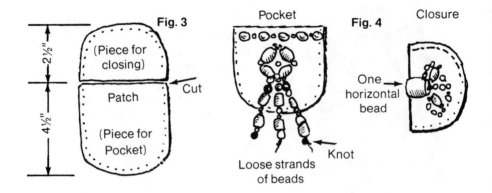

Fig. 3

(Piece for closing)

Patch

Cut

(Piece for Pocket)

2½"

4½"

Pocket

Fig. 4

Closure

One horizontal bead

Knot

Loose strands of beads

For a closure, make a decorative unit of beads and leather. Cut two leather patches approximately as shown (Fig. 3). With two-needle, direct-beading method, sew on an interesting arrangement of beads (Fig. 4). Use thread or decorative cord or yarn to string the beads. On each closure unit, place one large bead horizontally for inserting thong. Add decorative beads around. Make decorative pockets by beading the larger patch piece and allowing some beaded strands to hang freely.

Try on the vest, and establish proper position of pockets and closure units. Pin in place.

Sew units to vest using holes along edges of patches (most come with stitching holes precut). Use a backstitch for best effect (see page 85). Seal edge of closure unit to edge of vest (Fig. 5) by applying fabric glue between with toothpick.

Cut a thong 18″ long. Tie knot in one end. Slip through horizontal bead (Fig. 6). Repeat on other side to complete closure. When wearing vest, tie thongs in front.

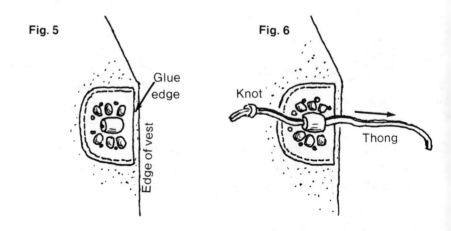

Fig. 5

Glue edge

Edge of vest

Fig. 6

Knot

Thong

The possibilities of creative combinations are limitless. Fig. 7 shows a few suggestions. Appliqué leather edges, or a collar shape. Bead around armholes, or make a decorative bead yoke, pockets or panels.

Use fake fur for lining. (If the edges are flush it will be reversible.) Add a trim of decorative cotton braid. Many fabric stores have a marvelous selection of these trims—many are of Indian-inspired designs.

Fig. 7

 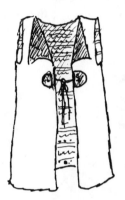

Beaded panels
Leather fringe

Appliquéd
leather

Decorative
fabric braid,
trims, yarn fringe

Decorative
buttons,
hanging beads
and fur tails,
rope fur trim
along bottom
edge

Sewn on beads,
hanging bead
strings,
beaded fringe

89

Hopi Dress

Traditionally, Pueblo women wore a garment made from a single piece of woven fabric about 40" x 48". It was tied or sewn over one shoulder and belted around the waist with many turns of a woven sash. It was a practical style, leaving one arm of the woman completely free for work. It used woven fabric exactly as it came from the loom. There were no raw edges. Bold geometric patterns were woven into the fabric.

A beach cover-up using the same basic construction can be quickly put together.

MATERIALS
Two bath towels (about 40" x 24"); one coat hook and eye; thong belt or woven tie sash.

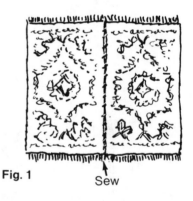

Fig. 1   Sew

Choose a pair of towels, with attractive patterns, that are not too heavy or thick. Sew the two towels together down one long side (Fig. 1).

Wrap towels around yourself, placing the seam under your left arm (Fig. 2). Have someone pull the two free upper corners over your right shoulder. Fold fabric under slightly below the left arm. Fasten sash or belt around waist and adjust garment as necessary. With safety pins, secure the two ends on top of right shoulder, pinning from neck out. This should leave 4" or 5" triangles unpinned. For shoulder seam,

90

Fig. 2

Fig. 3

Fig. 4

remove garment and sew together firmly alongside pins (Fig. 3). Remove pins. The triangular corners will fall gracefully over right shoulder. Wear towel robe this way, over the right shoulder, with entire right side open if desired. Hold in place by sash or belt. Or sew hooks at the hip to hold garment closed (Fig. 3). Another method of holding closed is to sew a small bone ring on each towel edge at hip. Slip a thong through the bone rings and tie (Fig. 4).

This is a quick way to make a bikini cover-up. Instead of terry towels, it can also be made of colorful fabric, to be worn perhaps over shorts or a body shirt. The side seam can be eliminated if the fabric used is wide enough.

To make this cover-up from fabric other than towels, cut a rectangle 4" x 48". Finish all edges. Pin and sew the shoulder seam as above. Sew hooks at hip and underarm of the open side.

To make this cover-up in maxi length, measure the extra length that would be needed according to your height. Cut fabric to the longer size. Finish edges all around. Sew shoulder seam and hooks as above. One leg will show—intentionally, of course.

91

Loin Cloth to "Minipron"

The loin cloth, breech clout or breech cloth was the primary male garment for almost all Indians until European influences began to affect their clothing styles. The loin cloth is basic, using simply a piece of material that is passed between the legs and up to the waist in both front and back, fastened under a belt and the loose ends allowed to hang down apron-like. It was adequate attire in all warm climates.

Leggings, when worn, were suspended from the same belt. Since the leggings were separate cylinders of fabric or hide for each leg, there was no actual "seat of the pants."

Loin cloths were rarely decorated, and frequently were made of inferior cloth. It was a strictly functional garment and, worn with a long shirt or upper garment, was often completely covered.

A decorated adaptation of the loin cloth becomes a "now" style for today's girls to wear as a bright accessory over jump suits, pants, or short, short pants. It's not really a breech clout, nor is it an apron; let's call it a "minipron."

In this adaptation, two fabric panels are suspended, front and back, from a belt. And we will decorate it elaborately, using an inspiration from a Penobscot beaded design. Since beading might be heavy or uncomfortable for a garment worn in this area, soutache braid gives somewhat the spirit of the beaded design of these Lakes and Woodlands Indians.

Most Indian motifs were geometric, and based on straight lines. However, the Lakes and Woodland tribes used graceful curved designs based on floral patterns. Although it was once believed such curving designs were European influences, recent archeological evidence has shown that curved line motifs based on nature objects were made by Indians of very long ago. Among artifacts that support this point of view are bird shapes of copper found in ancient mounds.

92

MATERIALS

½ yard fabric, of fairly firm texture such as velvet, suede cloth, fake leather, cotton, etc. (choose a color that goes well with the shorts it will be worn over); seam binding to match fabric; two packages soutache braid (color contrasting to fabric); small vial of seed beads; fabric or white glue; tissue or tracing paper.

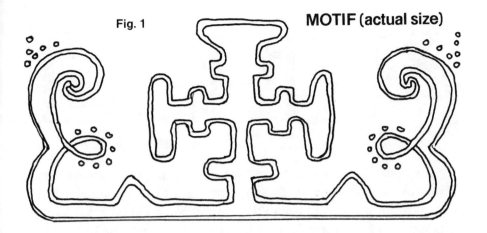

Fig. 1 MOTIF (actual size)

For design, trace motif (Fig. 1) onto light weight tissue paper. (Ignore the dots for now.) Trace motif twice more alongside the first motif, leaving about ½" between them, to get a border about 15" wide composed of three repeat motifs.

Cut fabric into two pieces 15½" x 16½" long. Pin the tissue paper to right side of one piece of fabric. Edge of motifs should be about 3¼" up from the edge and centered on 15½" width of fabric panel. Baste tracing paper to fabric around area of motifs (Fig. 2).

To decorate, sew soutache braid to fabric, following the design and stitching through tissue paper. Put a dab of glue on the cut end of braid to keep it from raveling. Lay soutache braid over design line on tissue paper. Using thread to match braid, start from wrong side of fabric, knot thread and bring it up. Take first stitch straight down about ¼" from where it came up, going through the braid and tissue paper into fabric. Then bring thread back up to right side of work. For next stitch, and each succeeding stitch, go down slightly behind previous stitch (Fig. 3); this is a backstitch. Keep stitches small and in center line of the soutache braid and they will not show.

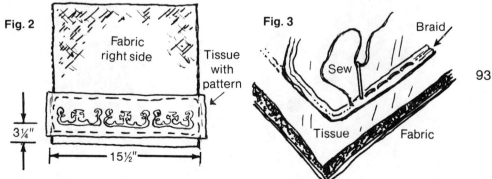

Fig. 2

Fabric right side

Tissue with pattern

3¼"

15½"

Fig. 3

Braid

Sew

Tissue Fabric

93

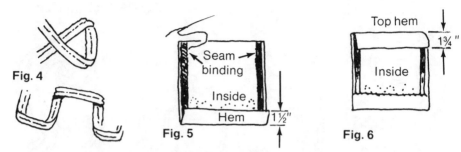

Fig. 4

Fig. 5

Fig. 6

Start in corner of one motif and sew braid completely around motif. To make loops or corners, fold or turn braid to follow design neatly (Fig. 4). When you get back to the starting point, cut off braid so ends ·will butt or meet exactly. Sew butted ends down firmly, and add a tiny dab of glue where ends meet.

Repeat for other two motifs. After all braid is sewed on, gently pull tissue paper apart and remove all pieces of it. Decorate the back or second piece of fabric in same way, if desired, or leave it plain.

Complete decorations by sewing seed beads to the fabric one at a time as shown by the dots on the pattern (Fig. 1).

To finish minipron, sew matching seam binding to long sides, turn inside and hem. (Fig. 5). Turn up bottom edge (below border) 1½". Fold raw edge under ¼" and make a hem 1¼" deep. Fold top down 1¾", turn raw edge under ¼" and baste. Machine stitch across top with thread to match fabric (Fig. 6).

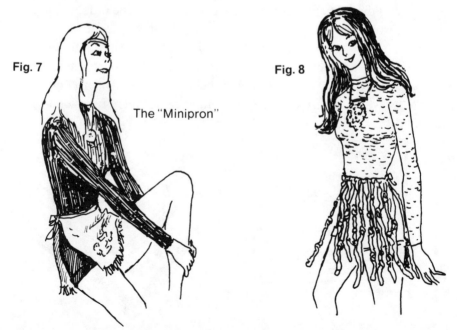

Fig. 7

The "Minipron"

Fig. 8

94

To wear, slip a cord or belt through top hems of both pieces. Tie around waist, allowing panels to hang down front and back. This "minipron" could be made in several variations. Use attractive patterned or textured fabrics and omit any added decorations. If you are sewing fancy pants, make a "minipron" to match. Or make "minipron" of fake fur and add a contrasting lining. Do one of leather with fringes; or of fabric with fur border sewn all around. You can buy fur edging or fake fur by the yard. Or add a border of yarn fringe (Fig. 7) or any desired braid.

The young girls of the Northwest tribes wore an apron-like garment that consisted mostly of thongs or thick handspun yarn tied to a cord at the waist. This, too, would be very effective over pants. Use nubby thick yarns, tie knots at various levels, and add some beads if you like (Fig. 8).

With these ideas and dimensions as a starting point, you can do your own thing. Try a "minipron" of crochet or macramé, making pieces each 15" x 16" and working belt to match. Fringe appropriately, of course.

Yoke Dress

Woman's garment
(Plains)

The everyday dress of most Plains Indian women was very simple, but garments worn for ceremonial occasions were lavishly decorated. The dress originally was made from two elk skins. When European cloth became available, the same basic pattern was followed, with the dress consisting of a long tube with a separate yoke section edged with fringe and decorated in other ways. The yokes of early skin dresses were frequently ornamented with quill embroidery. Later, color beadwork was used as trim on both skin and fabric dresses, sometimes covering the entire yoke. Leather strips hung with elks' teeth might be used in addition to or instead of beading. These dresses were generally midi length.

A simple "today" type garment that will fit almost any figure, inspired by the Plains dress, can easily be made.

Yoke Dress

MATERIALS

2 yards fabric in solid color 36" wide (or 1 yard 45" wide); 1 yard contrasting fabric for yoke (patterned, if desired); assorted beads or fringes (optional); felt-tipped marker; an old sheet or a large plastic trash bag.

When making any garment without a pattern it is a good idea to test the size and shape out first, using an old sheet or a large plastic bag, such as those used for leaves or garbage. (Don't put a plastic bag over the head, however; cut it open and use it flat as any fabric.) Use felt-tipped markers to indicate seam lines and cutting lines. Then use this for a pattern to cut good fabric.

For pattern for yoke, cut a piece of your test material 28" x 36". Fold in half both ways (Fig. 1). For head opening, cut a semicircle out of corner 3" across and 2" down as shown (Fig. 2). Unfold and cut slit about 3" down center back (Fig. 3).

Now put the piece on and mark front of yoke about 7" below head opening, or the length you prefer. This is the stitching line. It should be below the fullest point of the bust. Mark again 2¼" below this for fold and seam allowance.

Also mark with an X on yoke front the point under each arm where the underarm seam will be. This mark should be a few inches from your body for ease of movement, and should be level with seam line (Fig. 4).

96

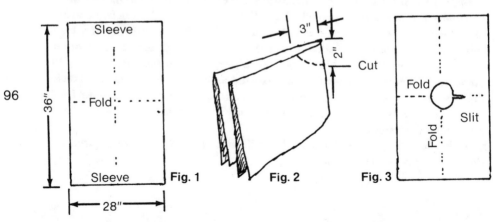

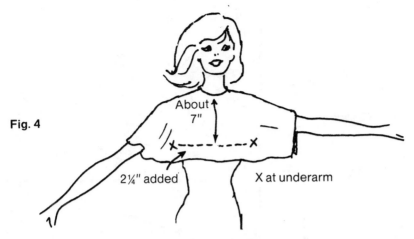

Fig. 4

About 7"

2¼" added

X at underarm

Take off yoke pattern. Fold it in half along shoulder line and mark stitching line, fold and seam allowance, and underarm seam locations on the back to match the marks on the front.

Fold yoke pattern in quarters and use felt-tipped marker to indicate stitching line, fold line, seam line, underarm seam, and 1" underarm seam allowance (as diagrammed in Fig. 5).

Cut 1" up along underarm seam allowance, cutting through all four layers. Now try yoke on again. On one sleeve mark a curved or pointed sort of shape to drape over and form a cape-like sleeve. Remove and cut sleeve edge (Fig. 6). Fold yoke pattern and cut other sleeve to match. The dimension of the bustline in front really determines the size of this dress. The yoke pattern is now completed.

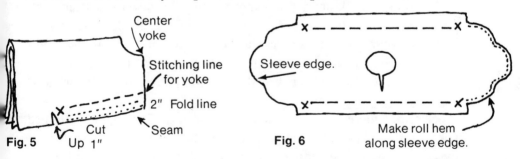

Center yoke

Stitching line for yoke

2" Fold line

Seam

Fig. 5   Cut Up 1"

Sleeve edge.

Make roll hem along sleeve edge.

Fig. 6

To make pattern for the lower or skirt part of the dress, measure distance between X marks on yoke pattern and add ⅜" on each side for seam (Fig. 7). This is the width of the skirt.

Decide on the length you wish for this dress. Make it mid-calf, knee length, modified mini, or whatever. However, if it is too brief it will not look well balanced with the wide yoke. Hold a tape measure from bustline to desired position of skirt bottom to determine length of skirt and

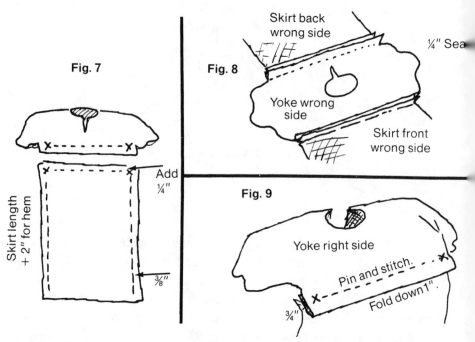

Fig. 7

Fig. 8

Skirt back wrong side

¼" Sea

Yoke wrong side

Skirt front wrong side

Skirt length + 2" for hem

Add ¼"

⅜"

Fig. 9

Yoke right side

Pin and stitch

Fold down 1"

¾"

¾"

add 2" for hem (Fig. 7). Using these width and length measurements, mark and cut two rectangular pieces of test material as diagrammed.

Get pattern ready for fitting by basting yoke to skirt front and back along seam lines, making ¼" seam on wrong side (Fig. 8). Turn right side out, fold yoke down over skirt 1", and pin stitching line (Fig. 5) to previous seam line (Fig. 9).

Pin front to back at each underarm point. Pin down side seams, allowing ⅜" seam allowance. Try on. Belt it in the middle to see how it shapes to your body. It is meant to be a loose garment. Adjust wherever necessary. When you are satisfied with the fit, remove pins and basting stitches so you can use the pattern pieces to cut your good fabric.

Select an interesting combination of fabrics. Combine a patterned yoke with a solid-color skirt, perhaps picking up one of the colors of the yoke design. The fabrics chosen should be of similar texture and weight. This dress could be made in a sturdy but not too heavy fabric, such as suede cloth. Or it could be made of a lighter, even a sheer, fabric. This creates a charming dress as the sheer fabric falls gracefully over the arms, forming a capelet or a butterfly sleeve effect.

Pin pattern pieces to fabric and cut out yoke and skirt sections. Use pins, pencil or tailor chalk to mark stitching and fold lines and X marks at underarm seam.

To finish neckline, use seam binding tape or make a tiny rolled hem. Sew snap or hook at top of neck slit. Hand sew a rolled hem along edges of sleeve (see Fig. 6). By hand or machine, sew up the 1" vertical underarm seams on yoke (Fig. 10), and side seams of skirt.

With right sides of both pieces together, sew skirt to yoke allowing ¼" seam, and matching side seams. Turn right side out and pin down the 1" fold-over. Pin stitching line to seam across both front and back of yoke. Top-stitch on stitching line (see Fig. 9) across yoke front and down each side on the vertical seam (Fig. 11). Be careful not to catch other layers in stitching. Repeat on back.

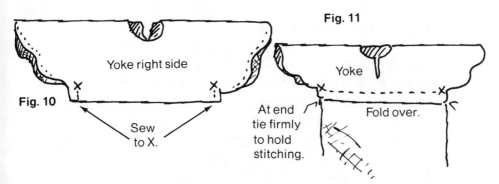

Fig. 11

Yoke right side

Yoke

Fig. 10

Sew to X.

At end tie firmly to hold stitching.

Fold over.

To complete this dress, turn up and hem bottom of skirt.

Make a matching sash of the same material used for yoke. Cut two strips 3" wide and 36" long. Seam together to make a strip 72" long. Fold in half lengthwise with wrong side out and sew a ¼" seam. Turn right side out and fold so seam is at center; press flat. (Fig. 12). Fold raw edges inside and sew ends. If desired, sew in a fringe before sewing ends.

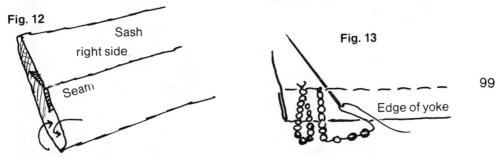

Fig. 12

Sash right side

Seam

Fig. 13

Edge of yoke

99

Turn in edges, sew by hand.

The decoration of this dress is up to you. Here are some suggestions inspired by actual Indian garments:

Add seed beads by sewing them over the printed pattern on the yoke. You can emphasize a part of the pattern, or bead over the entire design.

If you like to embroider, use colorful threads to accentuate pattern elements. Use embroidery floss on cottons, crewel yarn for heavier or nubby fabrics.

Fringe can be cut from felt or leather and sewn to underside of the folded-over bottom edge of yoke. Or a fringe of beads could be added by stringing seed beads and secure by stitching in at the yoke stitching line (Fig. 13). On heavier fabrics, upholstery or other ready-made fringes can be very effective.

To decorate the skirt, cut pattern motifs from scraps of the yoke fabric and appliqué at intervals. Sew cords, thongs, or strings of beads to hang from the center of this motif (Fig. 14).

Sometimes, the completed dress looks more Victorian than Indian. Either way it is charming. The color and texture of the fabric and type of decoration chosen determines whether it retains the feeling of the Plains Indian original (Fig. 15). Made of a suedecloth in natural or earth colors and elaborately decorated with beads and leather fringe, this yoke dress will strongly recall the ceremonial dresses worn by generations of Plains Indian women.

Fig. 14   **Fig. 15**

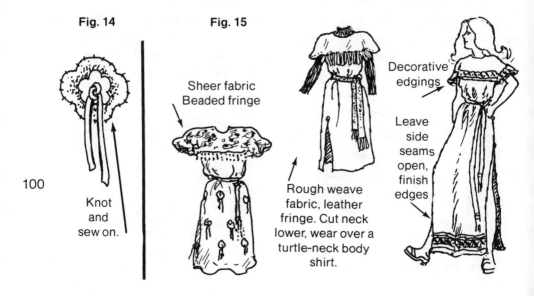

Knot and sew on.

Sheer fabric Beaded fringe

Rough weave fabric, leather fringe. Cut neck lower, wear over a turtle-neck body shirt.

Decorative edgings

Leave side seams open, finish edges

100

Fur Poncho

The classic Indian robe-blanket resembled a poncho although it was never called by that name. By cutting a slit for the head, the arms were left free.

Rabbit skins were processed into warm robes by the Indians of the Southwest and East. Strips of rabbit skin were rolled to make fur cords used to weave into blankets, which were warm and soft on both sides. As many as 200 rabbit skins were needed to make such a robe.

Inspired by the thought of such soft fur warmth, how about a poncho of fake fur?

MATERIALS
9 skeins of rug yarn; 2 yards of fake fur (plush) usually 64" wide (minimum 40"); large (K) crochet hook; felt marker; tape measure.

The basic structure for this poncho is a crocheted mesh with fur strips woven through. The cheapest grade of a fake fur can look elegant with this process. Matching the yarn to the fur gives the most elegant effect, but contrasting colors can also be effective. The choice is yours. The yardage of rug yarn skeins varies but 9 skeins should be adequate.

101

Only two basic crochet stitches are used, the double and single crochet and chain stitch. If you don't know the basics of crocheting, the diagrams on the following pages should be sufficient to get you started. Try a few inches to practice and learn how to make the basic stitches.

THE BASICS OF CROCHETING

**Diagram 1;
To start**

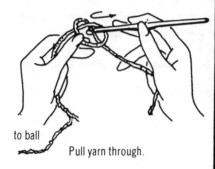

to ball

Pull yarn through.

**Diagram 2;
To Control Tension**

Wind on left hand.

Diagram 3: To Chain

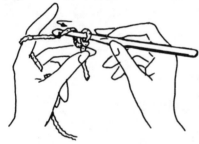

Wrap yarn over hook, catch and pull through, repeat.

TO SINGLE CROCHET

Diagram 4

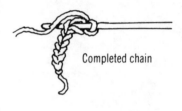

Completed chain

Insert hook through yarn of second chain from hook.

Diagram 5

Loop yarn over hook, catch, pull through chain: forms 2 loops on hook

Diagram 6

Loop yarn over hook again, catch and pull through 2 loops (leaving one loop on hook)

Diagram 7

Continue single crochet, going into next chain each time.

Diagram 8

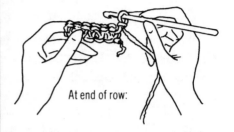

At end of row:

After last single crochet, chain two, turn crocheted piece around, crochet back into top of previous single crochet.

TO DOUBLE CROCHET

Diagram 9

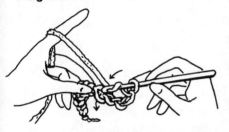

Chain length needed. Chain 3 extra, loop yarn over hook first, then go through 4th chain from hook, loop yarn over, catch and pull through making 3 loops on hook.

Diagram 10

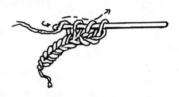

Catch yarn again, pull through 2 loops...

Diagram 11

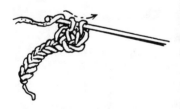

Catch once again, pull through 2 loops leaving one loop on hook; repeat, going into next chain each time.

Diagram 12

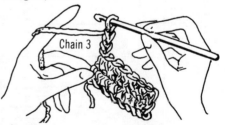

Chain 3

At end of double crochet Chain 3, turn piece around.

Yarn over hook, then insert hook through 1st double crochet in row below. Catch yarn, pull through 2 loops, loop yarn over and draw through. Continue...

103

Fur Poncho

To make a practice mesh: start by crocheting a chain several inches long. "Chain four" on end of chain made and turn over. Make a double crochet back into end of the chain (Diagram 9). Pull through twice completing a double crochet (Diagram 11). Chain one. To make next double crochet, skip a chain stitch, go down into the next one (Fig. 1). At end, chain 4, turn over and go back across again, making each double crochet directly above the previous double crochet (Fig. 2). Chain one between each double crochet to form opening for weaving.

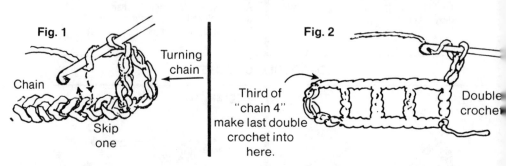

Fig. 1

Turning chain

Chain

Skip one

Fig. 2

Third of "chain 4" make last double crochet into here.

Double crochet

Continue to other end. The last double crochet is made into the third stitch of the "chain 4" you made to turn previous row. After the last double crochet, chain 4, turn and repeat across.

When you feel you have mastered making the mesh, unravel yarn and start your poncho.

Original chain should be 40″ long. Chain 4, and start making the mesh. Continue row upon row for a distance of 21″ (Fig. 3).

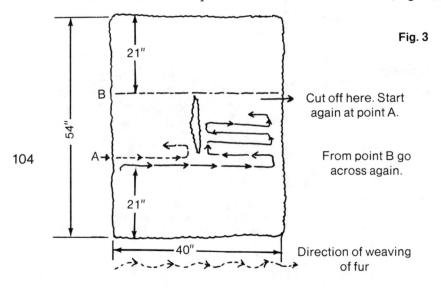

Fig. 3

21″

B

54″

A→

21″

40″

Cut off here. Start again at point A.

From point B go across again.

Direction of weaving of fur

To make neck slit, continue next row going only half way across (about 20"). Continue making the mesh this width for 12". Break off yarn, pull through last loop. Tie yarn on at other side point A. (Fig. 3). Start again, crocheting more mesh for 12". Then crochet the mesh all across (line B) for another 21" to finish remaining body of poncho.

When you finish a ball of yarn, tie on end of next ball and continue. Ends will be hidden in weaving or can be clipped off when finished. When mesh is completed to size shown, cut off yarn, pull through loop.

Now comes the weaving.

Turn fur face down and mark on the back using a ruler and felt marker. Strips should be about 1½" wide. This may vary with fur thickness and size of mesh you have made, try one piece first. Make strips 42" long for body of poncho, 22" long for each side of neck opening. Check widths and count your mesh rows to determine how many you will need. Cut out some strips. Fold each strip in half lengthwise. Weave over and under each double crochet (Fig. 4). Weave next strip across going under and over in reverse sequence for basket weave effect. Cut more and continue weaving until entire mesh is filled. Leave ends hanging.

Lay on a flat surface. Adjust fur and yarn so tension is even and it will lie flat. Check size and adjust so it makes size planned. Try on and adjust, if necessary, so weaving looks even. Make sure size is correct.

Lay flat again and trim off excess fur at edge, if any. Using matching thread, sew fur to crocheting as you trim (Fig. 5). Sew down fur at each end, thus finishing all edges and neckline.

Fig. 4

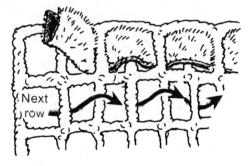

Next row

Fig. 5

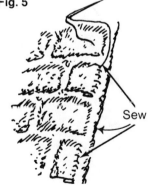

Sew

105

A fringe can be added, if desired, (see page 85), but it will require considerably more yarn.

Slit can be worn across neck (Fig. 6), or down (Fig. 7). Weave in a tie of yarn to hold neck closed.

This is an exceptionally warm, soft and unique cover-up.

Fig. 6

Fig. 7

Seminole Piecework

The Seminole Indians developed a unique and highly decorative technique of piecing together small bits of fabric. Woven cotton fabric was a luxury, obtained by trading with the Europeans. Seminole piecework probably resulted from a thrifty desire to make use of even the tiniest scraps of precious cotton fabric.

The women wear long full skirts consisting of bands and bands of piecework, shirts trimmed with bands of piecework, and a poncho-like cape, often of sheer fabric, with pieced bands along the edge. Over all this the women lavish as many strings of beads as they can afford. Seminole men wear pants and shirts, both decorated with bands of piecework.

The method of fitting or angling the pieces together looks intricate, but it is much easier than it looks. Once you know the process you'll find you can create decorative piecework trim for all sorts of uses. (The bands shown here are not quite as intricate as those of the Indians.) A sewing machine is a great blessing to have for this project; and since Seminole women now depend on them, machine stitching is quite authentic.

Although the Seminoles used only solid colored fabrics, there are so many exciting cotton prints that can be used too. Why not get off to a dramatic start by making a Seminole-inspired maxi shirt? Or, if you prefer, start small with the projects on page 218 while you learn the technique.

MATERIALS

Scraps and pieces of cotton fabric —all of similar weight (minimum size 4½" square); several ¼-yard lengths of new fabric of the same weight, the amount depending on how much left over fabric is available (choose solid colors and small all-over prints.) You also need ½ yard black cotton fabric; bias binding (assorted colors) in the following widths: 2 packages ½" wide, 5 packages 1" wide (black plus four colors), 2 packages 1½" wide; wide elastic.

107

The skirt is a dirndl style, made of a combination of a patchwork panel of large squares of fabric and two panels of the Seminole-style piecework, set off by two bands of solid black fabric. Let's learn the technique for making these piecework panels first.

The bottom piecework panel is made from three strips of 1″ wide bias binding and a strip of patterned fabric cut 1½″ wide. If the pattern is striped, it is easy to cut it evenly. Strips should all be about the same length, or 1½ times the circumference of the skirt. For a skirt 56″ around, seam strips to get a length of about 90″.

Sew patterned fabric strip (1½″ x 90″) to one color of the 1″ bias tape, making a ¼″ seam along one fold of tape. Sew 1″ bias tape in another color on the other side of patterned fabric strip. Sew on a third color of 1″ bias tape, matching bias folds, to last tape added. You will now have a piece of four contrasting colors, 90″ long and 4½″ wide, including two ¼″ folds on outside bias tapes. Turn to wrong side and press seams open (Fig. 1).

Measure and cut through all four strips to make pieces 1½″ wide. After you have cut several of these, pin them together, offsetting one color each time (Fig. 2) so that the stripes form a diagonally stepped design. Pin together and sew making ¼″ seams (Fig. 3). Continue until panel is desired length.

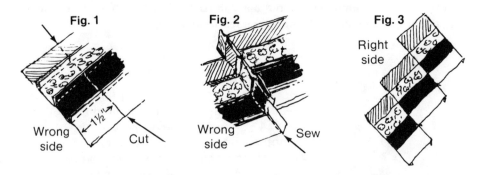

Fig. 1 Wrong side — 1½″ — Cut

Fig. 2 Wrong side — Sew

Fig. 3 Right side

Place pieced panel in front of you so that it looks like a band of diamond-shaped patches, with triangular corners of each row sticking up. Press seams flat. Measure and cut a piece of 1″ wide black bias binding 56½″ long. Pin one fold of binding to edge of piecework band and sew seam so the top points of second row of diamonds touch the binding fold, and the triangular tops of the first row of diamonds are caught in the seam edge of black binding. The right side should look like multicolored diamonds with a horizontal black border (Fig. 4) on top.

Fig. 4

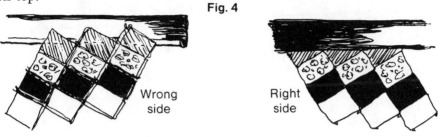

Wrong side

Right side

Similarly, seam bias binding in a contrasting color to the lower edge, catching triangular corners of bottom row of "diamonds" in seam (Fig. 5). Sew contrasting binding or fabric (cut 56½" x 1½") above the black band (Fig. 7, bottom), making ¼" seam. This is the first piecework panel.

Fig. 5

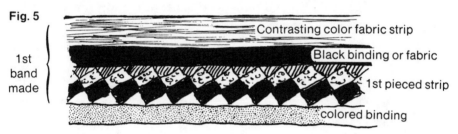

1st band made

Contrasting color fabric strip

Black binding or fabric

1st pieced strip

colored binding

The second piecework panel will have a different pattern because each of the four fabric or bias strips is of a different width. Select four bias bindings or ribbons in widths shown (Fig. 6), or any combinations of uneven widths. Cut (and piece if necessary) a strip of patterned fabric 1¼" x 90". Sew all four rows together, making ¼" seams as before. Press seams open. You should have a striped piece of fabric 90" long and 4¾" wide (including two ¼" seam allowances).

Measure and cut through all four stripes as before, this time making pieces 3" wide. To offset colors this time, however, choose the stripe of strongest color to follow (such as black in Fig. 6 and 7). Pin ¼" seams as before, having the corners of this dominant color stripe meet each time. Follow this alignment to sew the pieces together.

109

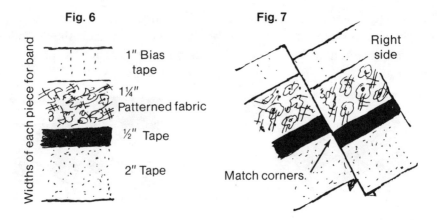

Fig. 6

Widths of each piece for band

1" Bias tape

1¼" Patterned fabric

½" Tape

2" Tape

Fig. 7

Right side

Match corners.

When finished, the second piecework panel will also have triangular points sticking up. Seam a contrasting color of ½" bias binding across the top, catching the triangles in the seam as before (Fig. 8). Seam the lower edge of the second piecework panel to the top row of binding on the first piecework panel.

Cut black fabric 56½" x 3½" (or seam together two pieces 28½" x 3½"). Join black strip to top of piecework with a ¼" seam (Fig. 9). You now have a skirt section over 12" long and 56½" wide.

The top of the skirt will be made of ordinary square-type patchwork. (Of course, if you'd like to make it entirely of piecework panels, and find it fun to do—keep on piecing and joining until you have enough for the entire skirt).

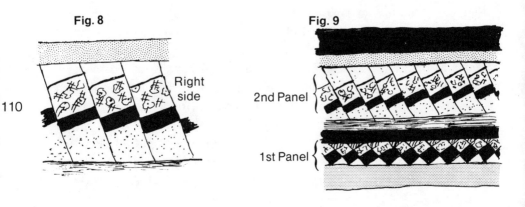

Fig. 8

Right side

Fig. 9

2nd Panel

1st Panel

Cut a paper pattern 4½" x 4½" for patchwork squares. Each patch is 4" square with ¼" seam allowance all around (Fig. 10). Cut 70 squares from fabric scraps. Small prints are particularly effective.

Start to assemble squares by placing a light square and a dark one (or any two contrasting squares) together with right sides facing. Sew ¼" seam down one side (Fig. 11). Repeat, pairing off all but 14 of the squares. Next join two pairs together, alternating contrasting ones, and add one more square to end of strip to make a unit five squares long (Fig. 12).

Then place two five-square strips together, alternating light and dark for contrast wherever possible, with right sides facing. Match up seam lines and sew across, making a ¼" seam. Continue joining 5-

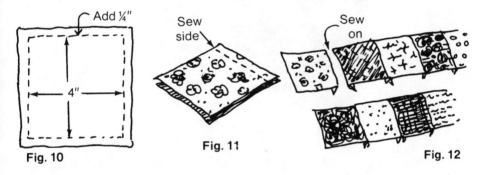

Fig. 10

Fig. 11

Fig. 12

square strips until you have a patched fabric piece 20½" x 56½". Seam one long edge of patchwork to the black fabric on top of the piecework band.

Hold top of patchwork to your waist and see how much longer than the bottom of the piecework band the skirt should be. Seminole women wear theirs down to the floor, but you might prefer ankle or maxi length. Determine how many more inches of skirt you need, add 2½" for hem allowance and ⅜" for seam allowance. Cut black fabric this wide and 56½" long. Sew to bottom band with ⅜" seam.

For waistband, cut black fabric 56½" x 3½" (or seam together two pieces 28½" x 3½"). Join to top patchwork with ½" seam. Close up back of skirt with ⅜" seam, sewing straight up from bottom to within 1" of top of waistband. Fold waistband over to wrong side, fold edge up ¼" and stitch fold to seam line (Fig. 13), creating a channel for elastic. Measure waist, add 1" and cut elastic to this size. Put a large

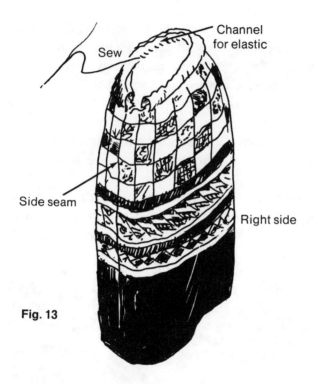

Channel for elastic

Sew

Side seam

Right side

Fig. 13

safety pin in one end of the elastic and push it through channel, securing other end of elastic to waistband with a pin so it will not pull out. Overlap ends of elastic 1″ and sew firmly together. Close up inside seam of waistband.

Pin hem and try skirt on. If necessary, unpin and adjust hem until it's just the length you'd like. Sew hem. Your Seminole-style skirt is now complete.

This skirt could be maue fuller, 60″ or 64″ around, by adding an extra row of 4″ squares to the patchwork and 4″ extra to the piecework panels for each additional 4″ in width. The length could be maxi, midi, or short, whatever you'd wear. A mini made entirely of piecework panels, without patchwork, would be attractive.

Once you have mastered the piecing process you can make these decorative panels and use them wherever you like, perhaps for an apron, or to lengthen a skirt or a dress. Try bands of piecework on the bottom of pants or dungarees, or make a long narrow piecework strip backed with grosgrain ribbon for a belt.

ꟷWeaving

Navaho weaving

Textiles were produced by certain tribes as early as 1,000 B.C. A variety of techniques were employed to produce material for clothing before textiles became readily available. Twining and plaiting, knitting and crocheting, finger weaving and, in the Southwest, loom weaving were all practiced according to the materials available. Spinning was done by hand or on a spindle.

A number of different types of fibers were used for textiles. Cotton was raised by Indians in the Southwest, but other tribes used reeds, grasses, cedar roots and the inner bark of trees. The hair of animals was used frequently: buffalo, mountain goat and moose were among the wild animals whose fur was processed into yarn; dogs were bred for their hair by Indians along Puget Sound; and the Spaniards introduced sheep in the Southwest.

Today the Hopi and the Navajo are considered the best weavers. The Navajo have raised sheep as a source of wool for their blankets since the Spaniards first introduced sheep and use a large vertical loom which makes it possible for them to weave quite rapidly. With a little ingenuity, you can make a simple loom similar to the Navajo's vertical, or blanket, loom. The fabric that this loom produces will probably be crude or "homespun" looking, but that can be charming in this age of machine-made perfection.

MATERIALS
18" x 28" (approximately) old frame or stretchers for artist's canvas (available in art store); three dowels about 20" long and about ½" diameter; one flat stick, 20" long, ¾" or 1" wide and about ¼" thick (A); a flat stick about 12" long and 1" wide (simple wooden ruler or paint stirrer will be fine) (C); four "C" clamps; ball of string or mercerized (crochet) cotton for warp; heavy knitting yarns as needed for background and pattern (weft); sturdy cord or string to attach the loom part to the frame and to thread the heddle; sturdy old table fork.

113

BASIC LOOM

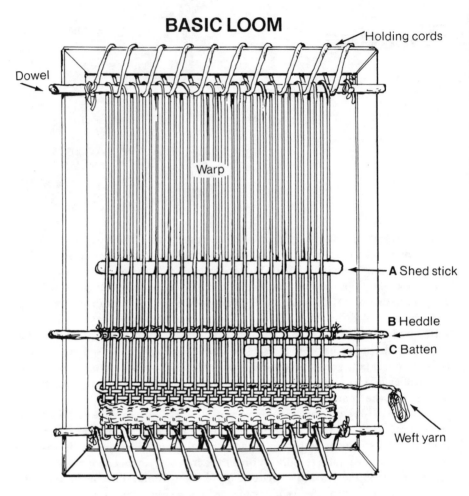

Holding cords

Dowel

Warp

A Shed stick

B Heddle

C Batten

Weft yarn

Weaving Definitions

WARP: The fixed vertical threads

WEFT: The yarn that is woven in and out of the warp horizontally (weft should be thicker than warp)

HEDDLE: A device to raise alternate threads of the warp

SHED: The space created when the alternate warp threads are raised

BATTEN: The flat stick inserted in the lower shed. When turned side-wise it opens up the shed more to allow the yarn to pass

114

How To Make a Loom

To make the frame, assemble the stretchers and make sure they are square and rigid. Glue the corners and nail on corner braces if necessary (Fig. 1). Using small "C" clamps, position dowels on to frame about 1½" down from each end (Fig. 2).

Wind on warp threads. It is easier with two people, one on each end. Make a ball of the mercerized cotton that will pass through the 1½" spaces allowed. Tie the end to one side of the top dowel. Go over the top dowel, down under bottom dowel, back up under then over the top dowel and repeat. This forms a continuous line forming a figure eight (Fig. 3). Setting up the loom this way automatically forms what is called a shed, creating alternate threads for weaving.

Space the threads about ³⁄₁₆" apart, filling an area on the dowels about 10" wide. Tie the end of the warp thread onto the dowel. With strong twine or cord, attach the dowel to top of frame by going back and forth up and over several times. Repeat on bottom, (see loom diagram "Holding Cords"). Remove bottom "C" clamps. If necessary, slightly tighten the holding cord on the bottom, to get a good tension to the warp. The warp should be firm but it should have some give, to allow weaving and movement of the heddle.

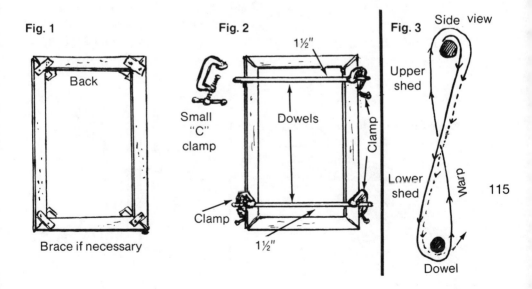

Fig. 1
Back
Brace if necessary

Fig. 2
1½"
Small "C" clamp
Dowels
Clamp
Clamp
1½"

Fig. 3   Side view
Upper shed
Lower shed
Warp
Dowel

115

The top "C" clamps can be left on to act as "feet" when used as a table loom.

Next, make the heddle that will allow alternating threads to separate as you work.

Slip the flat stick (A) through the upper shed that was formed as you threaded on the warp (Fig. 3). The remaining dowel will become the heddle stick (B). See diagram. Cut a yard or more of cord or string. Tie at the right side of warp. To make the heddle work, alternate warp threads have to be looped over the heddle stick (B) with enough room to allow opposite warps to be pulled up.

To do this: Move the shed stick (A) down towards the middle of the loom, and turn on its side, separating the warp. The warp threads that are now lower in the loom are the ones to be tied to the heddle. With your right hand, move the heddle stick across the top of the loom over the shed stick and warp. With your left hand, reach down, pulling cord under lower warp thread, pull up loop, give one twist to loop and push the end of the heddle stick through loop. Move both over next warp. Reach down and around next warp thread (lower level) (Fig. 5). Reach down, catch the cord, twist to loop, insert stick. Do it evenly and rhythmically all the way across until rod is completely inserted in the loops. Keep loops even and maintain the height established by the shed stick.

None of the warp threads should be disturbed by this process, the cord merely passes around them. When heddle stick is across loom with cord tied on, remove shed stick. Tie end of cord to heddle stick. Untie beginning of this cord from warp on other end and tie to heddle stick.

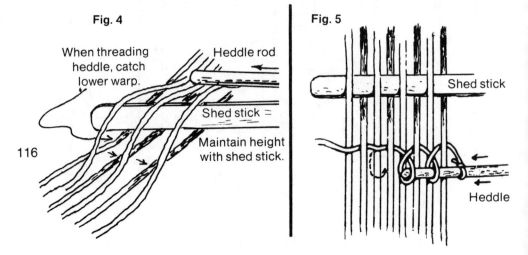

Fig. 4

When threading heddle, catch lower warp.

Heddle rod

Shed stick

Maintain height with shed stick.

Fig. 5

Shed stick

Heddle

116

Check to make sure sheds work properly. Slip out shed stick (A) and slide in again through upper shed near top of loom. Place a "C" clamp at center spot on each side of frame (Fig. 6) with heddle rod (B) resting against it. Now lift the heddle rod and place it on top of the "C" clamp. The alternate warp should raise up. Lower the heddle rod down to the frame, push the upper shed stick (A) down near the heddle. Turn the shed stick on its side. This should raise the opposite alternate warps on the lower portion of the loom. It's exciting to watch it happen! Now you are ready to weave.

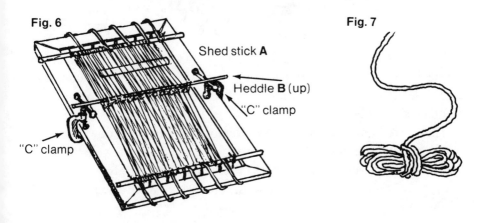

Fig. 6

Shed stick **A**

Heddle **B** (up)

"C" clamp

"C" clamp

Fig. 7

Make a small bundle of yarn (Fig. 7) by winding around fingers.

To weave, Step 1: slide A to middle, turn on edge. Slip batten (C) through below, stand on edge to allow ample room to slide yarn through. Push yarn bundle across (Fig. 8).

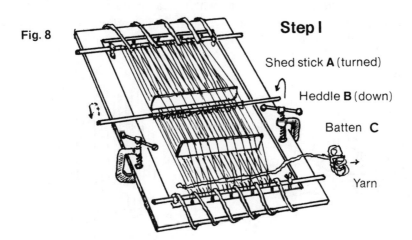

Fig. 8

Step I

Shed stick **A** (turned)

Heddle **B** (down)

Batten **C**

Yarn

117

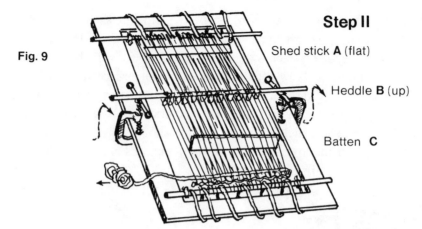

Step II

Fig. 9

Shed stick **A** (flat)

Heddle **B** (up)

Batten **C**

Step 2: Remove ruler (Batten C), lay stick A flat and slide up to top of loom. Lift up rod B (heddle) and place on props (clamps) at each side. Insert C, in shed now formed, turn on edge, pass yarn back to other side (Fig. 9).

These are the two basic steps. Remove C, drop B down against frame and slide A to middle and repeat step one. Every few rows, press weft down all across using the fork. Press gently but firmly so that weft tension is even and warp is almost obscured. Weft should not be crushed in.

Continue weaving back and forth. Avoid pulling weft as you work so tightly that it pulls against outer warp threads. Edge must be even, weave more loosely if it tends to pull in. This comes with practice.

Weave about ½" of one color, then make a stripe of another color.

To add this new color, cut off first color near middle, weave back through. Start new yarn weft somewhere near middle, weave through a few warps out to edge, then change shed and continue weaving as before (Fig. 10).

Fig. 10

Fig. 11

118

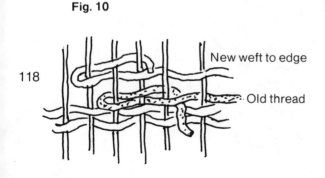

New weft to edge

Old thread

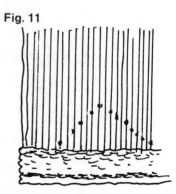

Use this method to add new weft yarn when a piece becomes too short, or when adding patterns. As work progresses, these ends are pushed down against weft yarn and held in position. Dangling ends can be trimmed off later.

Make several rows of stripes until you are familiar with handling the loom. Keep checking to maintain the 10″ width.

Now you are ready to incorporate a simple design like a triangle. With a felt marker, dot the warp threads to show where you want the triangle (Fig. 11). Weave background color up to the triangle corners.

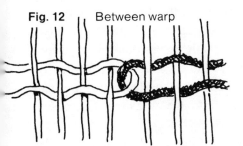

Fig. 12   Between warp

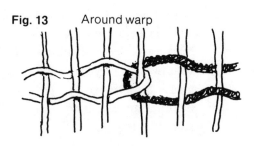

Fig. 13   Around warp

Insert new color (as for stripes) at area needed. Weave new color up to the background color and interlock the yarns (Fig. 12). Weft can be interlocked either between warp or around warp as shown (Fig. 13).

Start a new piece of background color on other side of triangle. Weave up to the color, interlock. Weave triangle color across. Weave background color on each side, interlocking with color on each side. Weave two or three rows with color this width. Weave next two rows, interlocking between another set of warp threads. Thus the background color comes in further and area of color triangle is reduced as you continue to weave up (Fig. 14).

Fig. 14

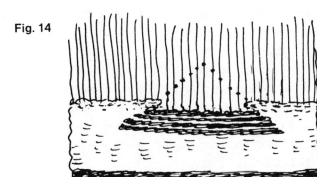

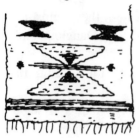
Fig. 15

Repeat patterns
for other end.

Continue, decreasing the number of warp threads covered by the triangle color and increasing the area of background, until the triangle reaches its point. Then return to weaving only background color again. Intertwining of yarns makes for a stronger fabric, and done consistently, makes a more even pattern. Now that you know the technique you can incorporate any bold design you desire into the weaving. For design ideas see Fig. 15.

When you are making patterns, there will be more and more bundles of weft yarn being worked at the same time, (Fig. 16). Let them hang down for use when needed.

As the weaving progresses, move the "C" clamps and heddle rod further up, as necessary.

When the woven piece is complete, cut the holding cords, and slide out bottom rod. With a tapestry needle, weave several rows of weft into the warp to replace the rod and finish the bottom of fabric.

Slip out the shed stick A and heddle rod B (now at top). Pull the cord that was on the heddle and it should pull right off the woven piece. The top of the fabric can be completed by tying warp threads in groups, like a fringe. The Indians often worked a piece up to the top rod, weaving in and out by hand once the shed stick and heddle rod had to be removed for space. This finished both ends.

This is a very primitive loom and the results are often uneven, but attractive weaving can be accomplished. Keep the design simple and watch the tension and evenness. Keep spacing the warp threads to maintain an even distance between them as you work. The Indians spaced the warp threads by weaving three cords through the warp as it passed around the top and bottom rods, securing each warp thread at an even distance from its neighbors (Fig. 17).

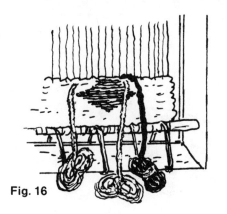

Fig. 16

Fig. 17

If you find yourself addicted to weaving—and it can happen—there are many good books in the library on weaving. This type of weaving in which the warp threads are covered is known as tapestry weaving. The warp threads do not contribute to the design. Look for further information for this tapestry type, or Navaho, weaving. Many commercial looms are available.

What can you do with the woven piece you have made? Show it to advantage. Make a simple bag (Fig. 18) or hang it like a sampler on the wall (Fig. 19). Smaller woven pieces can be used for pockets (Fig. 20), or for patches, or you might sew a panel to a tote bag. Attach several to each other and make a shawl or thick scarf (Fig. 21).

For a starter, the vest described in the next article can use hand-woven pieces.

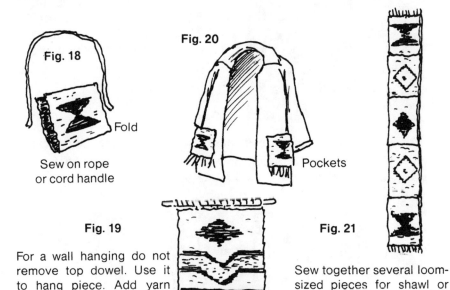

Fig. 18

Fold

Sew on rope or cord handle

Fig. 20

Pockets

Fig. 19

For a wall hanging do not remove top dowel. Use it to hang piece. Add yarn fringe.

Fig. 21

Sew together several loom-sized pieces for shawl or rug.

121

Hopi Inspired Vest

The man's "shirt" of the Hopi was often a single woven piece of material. The head hole was a slit left open as weaving progressed. Ends were sewn or tied at the side. It was similar to a poncho in some ways. When sleeves were added, a rectangle was laced onto each shoulder. There were no under arm seams (logical for keeping cool). Sleeves were sewn only at the wrists and the shirt tied at the waist.

From this shirt comes an idea for a "now" garment. Sometimes called a sandwich board vest, you can make it of two pieces of fabric you have woven yourself.

MATERIALS
Two handwoven pieces about 12" x 15"; two pieces of leather 1½" x 12" (or decorative ribbon braid); four 24" leather thongs or cords.

If you don't have handwoven pieces, any interesting fabric can be used. Upholstery samples might be effective. Cut 12½" x 15½", turn under edges and hem. Try a fake furry one.

122

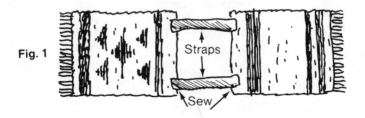

Fig. 1 — Straps — Sew

For shoulder straps, sew ends of leather to top corners of one piece and top corners of other piece (Fig. 1). For extra strength sew up in an oblong area and tie threads at ends so straps won't pull loose (Fig. 2).

For ties, fold cord or leather strip in half, pin to sides about 3" from bottom. Try on. Cords should be at waistline, adjust if necessary. Remove vest, sew cord in position (Fig. 3). Vest is complete, ready to wear over a simple pull over, shirt, or dress.

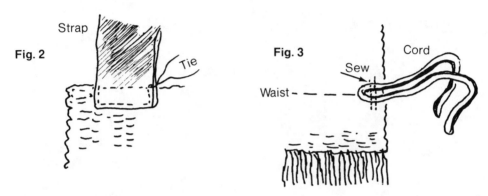

ᛘAdd-Ons

With what you've learned in these chapters, take off on your own tangents. Now you can enliven tired garments that are just occupying closet space. Or you can use these suggestions to finish off sewing in progress of your own.

Sew-Ons: Additions shown could be beadwork panels, direct beading strips, soutache designs (see page 93), embroidered decorations, hand-woven strips, or felt trims (page 170). You can purchase decorative

Square Neck Tops

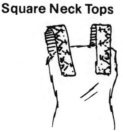

123

braids, many of which are definitely Indian inspired. Add trims to collar edges, pocket flaps—wherever a touch is needed. Sketched here are only a few of many possible ideas.

Pin trim on garment. Try on. Shift, juggle and re-pin, until the cut of the garment and the trim lines seem to agree. The inspiration for placing of trim may be Indian or your own creativity. When satisfied (check all angles), sew it all on carefully, using an appliqué stitch (page 85).

SEW ON: ← Beadwork   Decorative braid

V Neck Tops

Black velvet skirt, beadwork on velvet (see page 221 for suppliers of pre-beaded pieces) Add hanging bead fringe below.

Skirts, Pants, Sets

Add decorative braids

124

Add-Tos: Other additions need not necessarily be sewn or glued to the garment you wish to revive or give new personality. Collars, bibs, capes and trims can be decorated and worn over or tacked to the garment. The Indians had many such layered over adornments in a variety of interesting shapes.

Once you have decided on the shape of your collar, bib or whatever, it is wise to draw it on a piece of scrap fabric first. Cut out the shape and try it on. When you have made the necessary adjustments, you can then use this piece of material as a pattern to cut the shape from good fabric. You may then wish to make fringes of yarn, beads or leather (see page 85), or to add cords, thong or ribbons for ties.

Here are ways of incorporating special crafts and showing them off.

ADD TO:

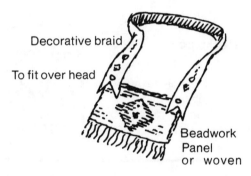

Decorative braid

To fit over head

Beadwork Panel or woven

Basically this is a rectangle, slit for head. Add beads or soutache design along edge, or weave a panel this shape leaving neck slit open.

Snap, sew or button together.

Bibs

sew

125

Direct beading with yarn fringes

Cord or leather tie. Panel hand-woven, beaded or felt designs

Chokers

Choker with added panel —make panels any shape.

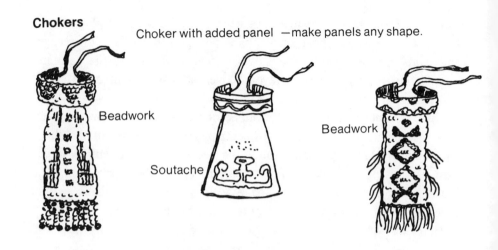

Beadwork

Soutache

Beadwork

Neckpiece

Neckpiece (chevron shape) Slip over ribbon or decorative braid

Beaded panel — or woven, crewel embroidered, crocheted, or macrame panel— whatever you like to do.

Waist Bands

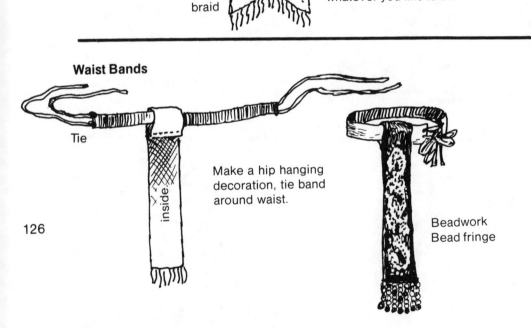

Tie

inside

Make a hip hanging decoration, tie band around waist.

Beadwork
Bead fringe

ACCESSORIES 3

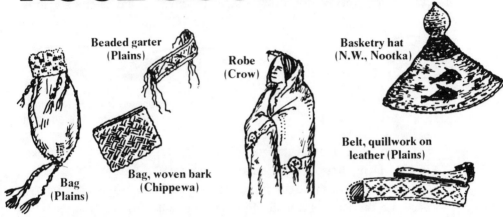

Beaded garter (Plains)

Robe (Crow)

Basketry hat (N.W., Nootka)

Bag (Plains)

Bag, woven bark (Chippewa)

Belt, quillwork on leather (Plains)

With today's styles, an accessory can be as far out as one's imagination can take it. Make something to be tied on, over or around you, or hung, draped or clutched.

For dances and ceremonial occasions, masks and headdresses were made by some tribes. Elaborate sashes, cloaks, garters, belled anklets, armbands, etc. had meaning in the ceremonies of various tribes. They are a source of inspiration for many accessories.

For everyday use the Indians protected their feet with sandals, moccasins or boots where necessary. In favorable climates, nothing was necessary.

For warmth and protection from the elements, the ubiquitous robe or blanket was pulled up over the head. Some Indians wore a simple fur cap in bitter weather. The Eskimo invented the shaped and sewn-on hood or parka.

Most head coverings were not for practical purposes. Many would fall in the category of regalia, to hold feathers or for indications of rank or achievement. One of the most well-known headdresses is the war bonnet of the Plains Indians.

The tribes of the West, where basketry was so well-developed, used inverted baskets as hats. In the Northwest, baskets were so finely woven they were waterproof. True hats were made by this basket method, and were decorated with traditional animal motifs. This chapter has many suggestions for contemporary accessories with the charm of their originals.

127

Over and Around

You've probably learned enough crafts in the first two chapters to make many things. Accessories should be easy—there are so many methods and ideas to adapt.

Belts offer a variety of ways to exercise your creativity. They come in every size, every width, every shape. If you want fancy shapes, draw

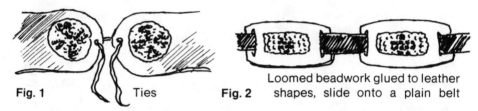

Fig. 1   Ties   **Fig. 2**   Loomed beadwork glued to leather shapes, slide onto a plain belt

a paper pattern first. Cut out of fabric, fake leather, suede, etc. (Fig. 1). Hem, line or bind edges. Decorate.

Beaded designs can be appliquéd to shaped belts (Fig. 1, 2) or used to decorate the ends of a sash (Fig. 3). Soutache designs (see page 93) are elegant on fabric belts, scarfs or sashes. Weave an armband or headband of beads or yarn on the beadwork loom. Add a band of Seminole piecework to the end of a sash or to border a square scarf. To wear a pieced band as a headband, line with a soft fabric.

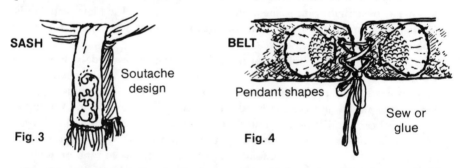

SASH   Soutache design   **Fig. 3**   **BELT**   Pendant shapes   Sew or glue   **Fig. 4**

Pendant ideas can be made up as pins. Put a pin on a hat or hold together a scarf with your creation. Some pendant ideas (see Chapt. 1) could be pieces sewn or glued to a dreary bag. Or make two shapes and attach to a plain purchased leather belt (Fig. 4).

Make scarfs and sashes to wrap around you, to encircle your hat, your neck, your waist. Tie your creation jauntily on a bag strap.

Basically, a scarf is a piece of fabric, cut and hemmed to a size you like. Check size of a favorite one in the closet. Then cut a piece of fabric and decorate it.

For a sash, figure the waist measure plus sufficient fabric to tie and hang down. Make as wide as desired. Add fringes (see page 85) or /and decorations. Make tiny sashes to tie around your arm, neck or hat. Use your tape measure to determine the correct size. Use a wild fabric and hem edges neatly. Even scraps and trims of all sorts can be turned into accessories that are as practical or as whimsical as your mood.

Sash — Woven plus Beads

Hopi and Pueblo Indians made attractive woven sashes for everyday use, elaborate ones for rituals and dances.

Woven sashes, using simple finger weaving of yarns, can be created on the handmade bead loom with beads adding an interesting note. The complete instructions for constructing the loom are on pages 22–23.

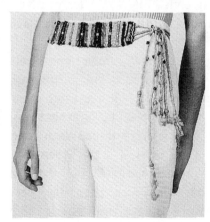

MATERIALS
Two skeins of wool knitting yarn, fairly firm, one ochre, one black (or colors preferred); two blunt yarn needles; a needle threader; pony or tile beads in complementary colors (such as black, orange, blue); homemade bead loom.

To string loom for sash, cut ten pieces of yarn (ochre). The length of each piece of yarn is your waist measure plus 45". These make the warp. Tie ends of yarn around the ice cream stick and roll up about 12". Clamp with clothespin onto one end of the loom. Bring the yarn up over end of loom. Spread across both springs, filling the width of the metal piece. Bring other ends of the yarn down over the other end of loom, wind them around another stick and pull tightly. Clip to hold in position (Fig. 1).

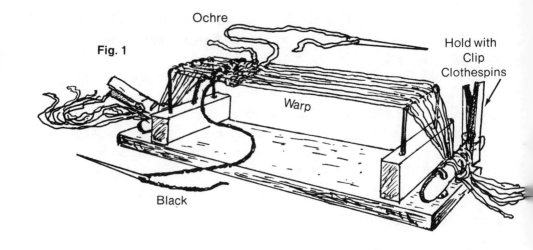

Fig. 1

Ochre

Hold with Clip Clothespins

Warp

Black

Tie a piece of black yarn at left top corner, and thread it on needle (needle threader is a big help). Weave the black yarn in and out of the warp going across and back. Thread ochre thread on needle, tie on at the right just below the black, leaving ends (Fig. 1). After you have some fabric made, ends can be woven into it. Weave ochre across and back.

String on a row of nine beads, one black, seven orange, one black. Hold the beads under the warp and run the needle with ochre yarn through beads over warp to hold beads in place (just as with loom beading). Beads can be laid above or below, depending on where your yarn is. Make sure yarn goes around outside warp thread each time.

Weave several rows of black, then several rows of ochre. Keep rows tight against each other as you go. Warp threads will not show in finished piece. The beads help maintain the placement of the warp and the width of the sash. As you weave, keep the yarn loose so that the width established by beads will not vary and woven part will not pull in between each bead row.

Add another row of beads. Weave black across and back, ochre across and back, alternating until you have three stripes of black. Weave about ¼" of black, add a row of beads (black beads with a center orange bead). Weave another ¼" black, three stripes, then about ½" of ochre. Make a row of orange beads, one black on each end, then weave another ½" of ochre. Repeat. (Fig. 2). This pattern can be repeated throughout the belt.

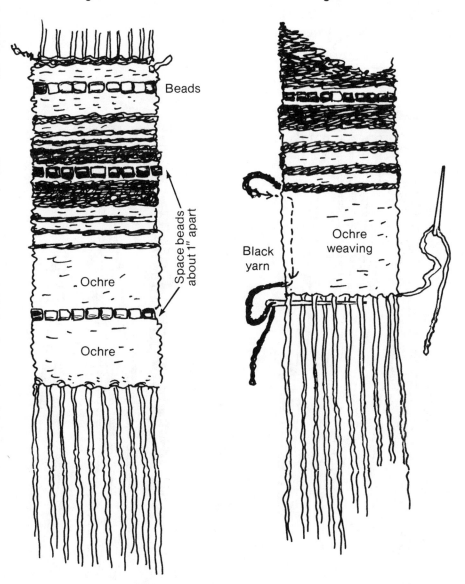

Fig. 2   Fig. 3

Beads

Space beads
about 1" apart

Ochre

Ochre

Black
yarn

Ochre
weaving

When a band has been worked in a second color, to reintroduce
the black, pick up the black threaded needle and run it inside, along
the edge of the new band of weaving, making certain that it does not
show. Bring out at the proper point and start weaving (Fig. 3).

All distances are approximate and variations give it a distinctive homespun look. In the center of the row of black beads, you might add other colors (blue or green, etc.) for variety.

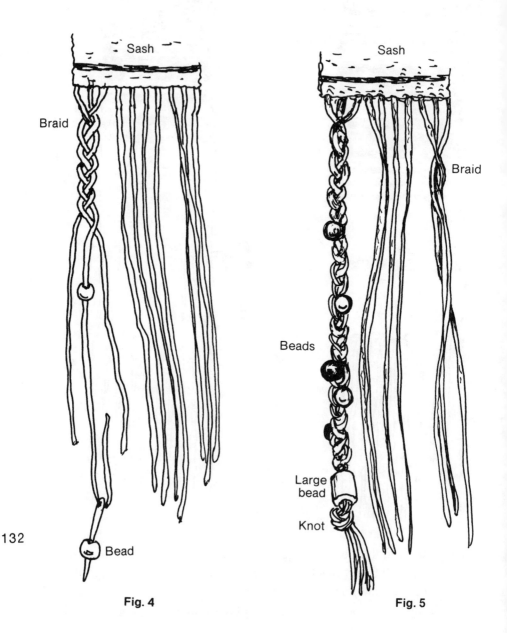

Fig. 4

Fig. 5

132

When coming to the end of a yarn piece tie it to the warp. Then weave the yarn up into the woven fabric to conceal the end.

To add a new piece of yarn, thread on needle, go through ¼″ or so of woven fabric, coming out at a point on the warp where new weaving will begin. Tie to warp thread and start to weave. Push all weaving together firmly as you work. Clip all ends when completed.

When sash fills the loom, roll the finished end around the stick unwinding new warp thread from lower stick to continue working. Hold end of woven section to top wire with clip clothespins. Rewind warp at the base of loom, and hold in place with clothespins.

Weave a strip about 6″ shorter than waist measure. Tie off the ends of the weaving threads and weave back up into fabric. Remove sash from loom.

For sash ties, divide the hanging warp, gathering three strands on each side (Fig. 4). (There will be four strands in the middle.) Tie a knot, then braid the strands on one side for about 10″. Thread one strand on yarn needle. As you continue, string on a bead, spacing at random. Continue to braid to within 3″ of end, adding beads occasionally. Tie knot. Slip all three strands through a pony bead. Tie another knot (Fig. 5).

Repeat with the three strands on the other side. In the center, braid the same way, doubling one of the braiding strands in order to use up four strands. Repeat on the other end of sash. Use glue on the inside pony beads, if necessary, to keep them from sliding off.

This sash can be made of any combination of colors, with any striped pattern desired. The dimension of the nine beads across determines the width and adding rows of beads, not more than 1″ apart, helps maintain an even width.

 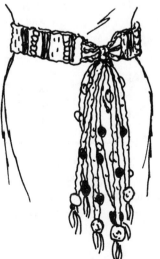 

Leather and Bead Belt Combo

Here is an easily assembled belt that combines beads with leather. Start your shopping in the stationery store! The secret: link pieces of leather with note-book rings. Few will guess its humble beginnings.

MATERIALS

Nine 1½" book rings; 8½" square piece of suede leather. firm but not too heavy (or a strip 1¾" x 32"); about 60 pony beads of two or three colors, such as blue, brown, and orange (or any beads with large holes: bamboo, wooden, macramé beads, etc.); epoxy or fabric glue; 60" cord or leather thong; masking tape; clip clothespins.

For the pattern of the leather shape, trace the outline (Fig. 1) on paper. Cut out. Trace around this shape on the wrong side of the leather with felt marker. Draw 8 of these shapes. Try to keep the same direction of the grain of leather on all pieces. Cut out the eight leather shapes.

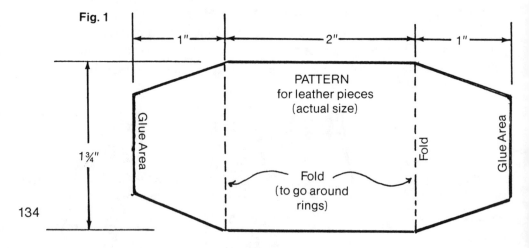

Fig. 1

— 1" —   — 2" —   — 1" —

1¾"

Glue Area

PATTERN
for leather pieces
(actual size)

Fold

Glue Area

Fold
(to go around
rings)

Open a ring and slide on eight beads. Separate them so that you have four on each side of the ring. Wrap end of a leather piece around the ring, between the two groups of beads, to check the size of the leather.

Temporarily tape leather in back. Repeat, placing eight beads on each of seven of the rings. Fold leather as shown to link each ring together (Fig. 2).

For the two end rings, slide 13 beads on each ring, arranging colors as desired, and close rings.

Try on the belt to check size. The two end rings should nearly meet in front. The belt is planned for approximately a 25″ waist. If the belt is too short, fold less leather around each unit (Fig. 2). If it is too long, fold more around the rings and trim the leather if it overlaps in back. If the belt is far too long, omit one unit and adjust the foldover of the remaining units. When the fit is satisfactory, remove the tape and prepare to glue.

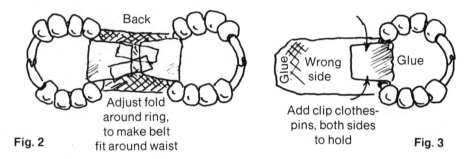

Fig. 2   Adjust fold around ring, to make belt fit around waist

Add clip clothes-pins, both sides to hold   **Fig. 3**

To assemble the belt, mix the epoxy glue. Spread glue at one end of a leather piece (wrong side) in areas indicated in Fig. 1. Fold the leather around the joint of ring, separating the beads, so that there are four at the top and four at the bottom of the link. Fold glued area against the center of the leather piece and hold closed with clip clothes pins on each side (Fig. 3).

Add glue to the other end of the leather piece, fold it around another ring and repeat. Continue gluing strips around links, ending with the thirteen bead rings on each end (Fig. 4). Allow the glue to set thoroughly.

135

Fig. 4   Belt (assembled)

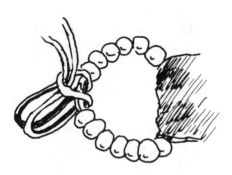

Fig. 5

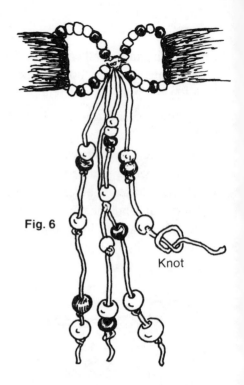

Fig. 6

Knot

To finish, cut a 30″ piece of thong (or cord). Tie between middle beads of end ring (Fig. 5). Repeat with the other ring. To wear, tie the cords together.

To decorate the cords, slip remaining beads over ends. If the ends fray, dip them in a little glue, allow to dry. Then beads will slide on easily. Try on the belt. Tie cords, and adjust the beads at various random levels so they hang attractively. Tie a knot below each bead to hold it in position (Fig. 6).

For economy, various other materials could be substituted, such as the fake leather sold for upholstery, or for covering chair seats. Fake leather (sometimes called expanded vinyl) usually has some sort of backing. Choose one that is heavy enough for body in the belt but not so thick that it can't be folded around the ring.

If you want leather, but find it hard to obtain, most stores carry suede elbow patches (in the notions department). This is an excellent weight for the belt. Buy one pair of the largest size available. Make the pattern piece 1½″ wide or slightly smaller, so that you can get four pieces from each elbow patch. Add more beads to each ring when assembling the belt so that the rings won't show or use smaller rings.

Patchwork Leather Belt

This project uses odds and ends of suede leather scraps to make a belt.

MATERIALS

Scraps of suede leather in various colors; strip of felt 3" wide by length determined by waist measure plus 6"; purchased buckle (or a used one from a worn out belt); rubber cement (usually comes with brush in jar).

Some shops or mail order suppliers have suede leather scraps to buy by the bagful. Or you may have your own scraps left from other projects. Two colors would do, but an assortment of colors is more fun. Light color suede can be dyed if you'd like more of an assortment of colors. If you have no access to leather, buy some chamois in the variety store and dye pieces in several colors. Use fabric dye as directed by manufacturer. Allow to dry, spreading it flat.

For the belt, make two paper pattern pieces (Fig. 1) in the sizes shown. Figure the size of belt you'll need. From this figure, determine how many pieces you'll need to cut. Each unit is composed of one large and two small triangles and adds up to about 1¾".

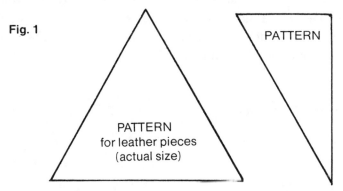

Fig. 1

PATTERN

PATTERN
for leather pieces
(actual size)

Cut out pieces in the quantities you have calculated. Cut a 2" x 3½" piece for the buckle end. Lay all the pieces on the felt strip the size of the belt and plan your color arrangement. Set the leather pieces to the side.

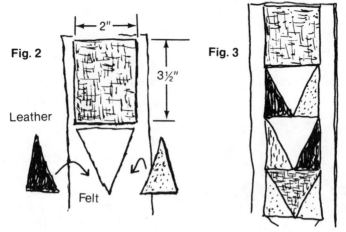

Fig. 2

Leather

2"

3½"

Felt

Fig. 3

To attach the leather to the felt, apply rubber cement to the felt, doing small portions at a time. Position the rectangular piece at one end of the felt (Fig. 2). Then start adding the triangular shapes as planned, fitting each triangle against the other so that no felt shows between. Arrange in a row down the center of felt. There will be a strip of felt on each side which will be trimmed later. Keep brushing on rubber cement and gluing down the triangles the entire length of the belt (Fig. 3).

Roll up a ball of dried rubber cement and use this to remove any excess cement that gets on the leather surfaces. Allow to dry thoroughly.

To make a wearable, durable belt, the edges of the leather pieces must be stitched with the sewing machine. Stitch around each piece. If you follow the arrow directions shown in Fig. 4 (A & B), you will cover each edge of one motif in continuous stitching without stopping.

When completely stitched, trim off the felt edges with scissors (or a knife if some leather needs evening up also). Be very careful not to cut into stitching.

138

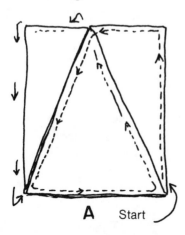

Fig. 4

A   Start

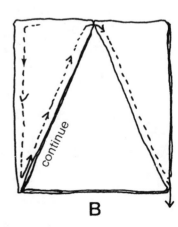

continue

B

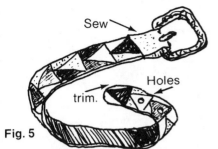

Fig. 5

Fig. 6

For buckle, cut a hole for the tongue in the end with the rectangular piece of leather. Use knife or punch. Slip the tongue of the buckle through the hole and fold the leather around the buckle. Sew to the back (Fig. 5). With an awl or a hole puncher, make holes at the proper spot at the other end of the belt so that it will buckle neatly. Round the corner of this end if desired.

This patchwork process for suede scraps could be used to get a solid piece of leather for any project. Random patchwork could use up all sorts of strangely-shaped scraps (Fig. 6). Cut and butt the shapes neatly. Make a bag, a gauntlet, or edge a vest.

Gauntlet

Here's a great put-on that displays your beadwork ability even if you only have the patience or time to make a tiny piece.

MATERIALS

2" square (or a circle) of loomed beadwork; 3½" x 7" piece of medium weight suede or other flexible leather; two yards of thong or cord; leather punch or awl.

Draw a 3½" x 7" rectangle on a piece of paper. Wrap it around your wrist and mark where it overlaps. Cut out a pattern, making it ⅛" less than the wrist circumference on each side. Curve the top edge slightly so that the ends are about 2¼" long. Your pattern should be the shape shown (Fig. 1). When the paper pattern fits properly, use it to cut out the leather gauntlet.

A beaded motif will be attached to the center of the gauntlet. If

139

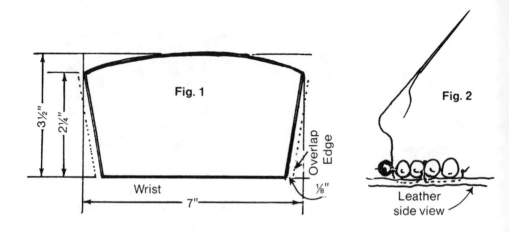

Fig. 1

3½"

2¼"

Wrist

7"

Overlap Edge

⅛"

Fig. 2

Leather side view

beading is not your thing, some stores and mail order suppliers (see p. 221) carry motifs already beaded (rosettes). The beaded end of a tired pendant can be rescued for this purpose.

Appliqué the beadwork to the leather, trying to go through only the upper layer of leather so that no stitching shows in the back (Fig. 2).

For ties, punch three holes along the edge of each short side of the leather with a leather punch or awl (Fig. 3). Work a 12" piece of thong or cord through each hole. If the thong is loose in hole, tie around. Generally the thong should fit firmly enough to hold as is.

To wear, tie each set of thongs and allow the ends to hang like a fringe (Fig. 4).

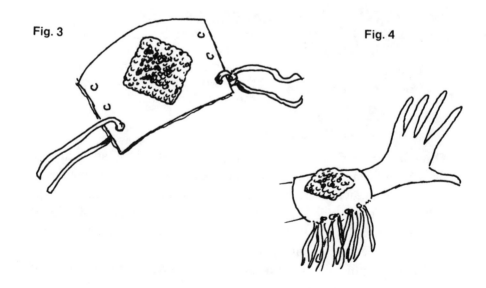

Fig. 3

Fig. 4

Wrist Wrapping

This quickly made wristlet features leather and beads.

MATERIALS

1½ yards suede leather thong; about 40 pony beads, color (or colors) preferred.

Use suede leather about ½" wide, sold for lacing. The pony beads should fit very snugly on it.

To assemble, slide beads onto the thong, spacing and varying colors at random (Fig. 1).

For tying space, leave an unbeaded area about 9" from each end. For decorative ends, slide on about nine beads, so that you have entirely beaded an area about 3½" from ends (Fig. 1). Put a dab of glue inside the last bead if necessary. Generally the leather will hold the beads firmly. If not, add a dab of glue any place it is necessary.

To wear: Wrap loosely around and around your wrist (about seven times). Tie the ends.

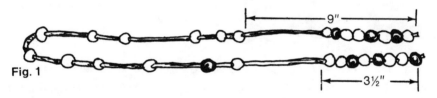

Fig. 1

For a different effect, if you are not exactly the leather type, make a wrapping of velvet. Use velvet tubing (available in fabric stores and notions), and barrel beads. To string, put some glue on each end of tubing. When it hardens, it will form a tip to slip on the barrel beads. To finish ends (Fig. 2), add more glue to each end of the tubing and slide end inside of last bead.

141

Fig. 2   Velvet tubing   Glue inside.

Potato Print Scarf

Stick bundles   Print   Rolled leather   Print

Most Indian decorations were woven-in or attached onto the garment. Applied designs were usually painted on the surface. In the Northeast, however, some designs were stamped on, for basket decoration.

Various materials were used to make the stamps. A simple, tied bundle of evenly cut sticks, a rolled piece of leather made interesting designs. Designs were cut into the surface of soft wood or a halved potato. For their stamp pad, the Indians used buckskin soaked in dye or the dye was spread on a fleshy leaf.

Exciting patterns can be created for today, using the same method. Make a scarf with several kinds of stamps to get the feel of the process, then add designs to whatever you wish.

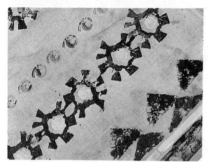

MATERIALS

Fabric (size for scarf); one or two colors of acrylic paint (available in art and craft stores); old brush; old dish or plate; sponge; scrap of leather; potato.

Select a fabric and cut it to the size desired for your scarf (measure a favorite one if in doubt). Save the scraps for practice pieces. Fabric can be any material with a fairly flat, firm surface, sheer or not. Pick a white material or one in a pale color, or dye a white fabric the background color desired. One or two deep colors stamped on a lighter color works best. Make it mellow and "woodsy" with brown and orange on yellow, or make it "now" with purple on pink.

Prepare the printing block. Cut the potato in half. Make a design on the potato, such as those shown, inspired by an Onondaga basket design. Cut away areas so that you leave a raised design (Fig. 1). Make cuts straight down, try not to undercut.

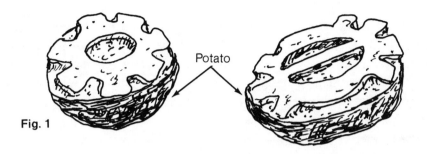

Fig. 1

Potato

For simple triangle stamps, cut the corner off an ordinary synthetic kitchen sponge. Try a leather stamp if you have a scrap of leather. Wet the leather, roll up and tie (Fig. 2). For straight lines use a small piece of wood (balsa is good). For dots, a cork is fine. Gather together what you plan to use.

Plan your overall design, where the repeats will be placed. It can be stamped on freehand if you like or you can draw it on paper (Fig. 3). Draw general circles where potato designs will go, triangles and lines can be drawn in place. Place the paper guide beneath the fabric if it is sheer enough to see through. If not, mark little dots lightly with pencil on the fabric, to guide you in placement of units.

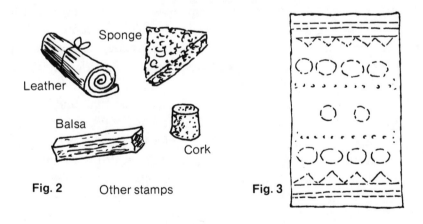

Leather

Sponge

Balsa

Cork

Fig. 2   Other stamps

Fig. 3

Now you are ready to decorate the fabric. On a flat surface, covered with newspapers, lay out the fabric. With thumbtacks or pins, tack the fabric flat. Wear old clothes or an apron so you won't spoil your clothes.

In a dish, squeeze out a dab of one color of paint. Brush it on the raised surface of the potato. Press down on a piece of scrap fabric to

143

see how it looks. Brush on again. Keep trying until effect is good: no globs of paint, clear design with a little of the fabric showing through. Paint should be transferred in a delicate layer, otherwise the fabric will become stiff in area of design. Then brush on paint again, apply the stamp to the fabric. Brush on paint, repeat each time until all units are in place.

For leather or cork, spread the paint in a thin layer in a dish, stamp down into the paint, then stamp onto the fabric. For sponge, dampen slightly with water, paint on the surface of the sponge or dip into a layer of paint and press down on the fabric.

Always test each stamp on a scrap of fabric when starting new design or color. Do all units of one color, then wash up everything thoroughly and start on the next color. The brush and dish must be washed immediately. *Remember:* this paint is very washable when wet, but once it is dry it is *very* permanent.

When the design is complete, allow it to dry thoroughly.

Sew a neat hem along the edges of scarf. Press on the wrong side. The fabric can be hand washed.

Stamping is fun to do. It takes a little practice to estimate the proper thickness of paint, the amount of pressure needed, etc., but as you work you will get a feel for the technique and you'll know. Fill up some scrap fabrics, such as an old sheet and you'll gain confidence and get the hang of it. Shapes or designs can be anything that appeals to you; a "love heart," paisley shapes, overlapping goemetrics, stars and moons, etc.

When you see the effects you'll think of something that could benefit from applied designs. Make a sash with decorative ends. Add a border design on the collar of a "nothing" type blouse. Just be very careful when decorating clothing that you let each section dry thoroughly before moving or turning the garment to do another section. Have your hands clean when handling the fabric. If you are not careful, the paint may be transferred to spots it should *not* be in. And we emphasize again that the paint is permanent when dry. With a little care and neatness, "potato" designs can cover whatever you wish.

144

Tote and Carry

Button Bird Tote Bag

The Indians of the Northwest coast used shell for inlays, jewelry and other ornamentation. Shells were converted into decorations, often by tedious processing. For special ceremonial blankets, sewn-on shells outlined designs of humans or animals. The design identified the family to which the owner belonged, so that the blankets were used for identification as well as for show of wealth or power. When trade goods became available, the Indians recognized the possibilities of substituting pearl buttons for the shells, and created the button blanket. The stylized human and animal figures used for the shell blankets were retained and simplified to suit the button medium.

On a smaller scale, you can make a tote inspired by button blankets of a thunderbird or raven design.

MATERIALS

½ yard black fabric (velour, velveteen, wool or sturdy dull-surfaced cotton); ½ yard bright red fabric (corduroy, canvas, or any sturdy material); 9" square of red felt (or scraps); buttons: about 200 of the white pearl type (shirt buttons) varying from ¼" to ½" diameter, one two-holed button about ⅝" for the eye of the bird.

The first step will be to gather buttons. Gather them from your friends, scour thrift shops, find a store that sells them by the bag or box. Collect a good assortment—two holes are better and quicker to sew on, but four holes are fine. Old are just as good as new. (For authentic buttons see suppliers page 221).

For the bag, cut piece of black fabric 12" x 24". Cut red fabric 15" x 31". For the handle of the tote, cut a black piece 2½" x 15" and a red fabric piece 5" x 15".

Decorate the black piece first, before assembling bag. The button design will be applied on the upper part of the black section (Fig. 1).

The patterns on pages 146-147 show solid areas to indicate red felt appliqués. Trace these areas on small separate pieces of paper and cut them out of the red felt. The eye is a solid red unit; a button will be sewn over it (Fig. 2).

145

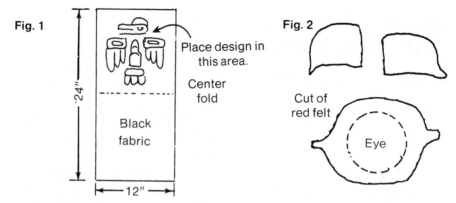

Fig. 1

'24"

Place design in this area.

Center fold

Black fabric

|←— 12" —→|

Fig. 2

Cut of red felt

Eye

On a piece of tracing or tissue paper trace the bird pattern given (half the body plus head). For button placement draw along the solid center lines. You needn't indicate each of the buttons. Do, however, indicate the red areas. To draw the other half of the body and other wing of the bird, fold the tissue paper along the center line and trace on the other side of the paper. Open up the tracing paper for the bird body shape. Center head pattern over body drawing, trace in position. Pin the pattern to one half of the black fabric. The lines of the wing edges should be about 1″ from each side, the top of the head about 1¼″ down from top.

Using a tracing wheel and a transfer sheet, indicate the areas where red must be placed. Remove the sheet. Glue or appliqué red felt pieces in areas indicated. (See page 85 for appliqué).

BUTTON TOTE PATTERN

Head Pattern

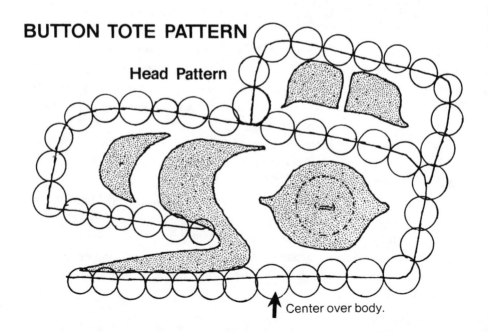

Center over body.

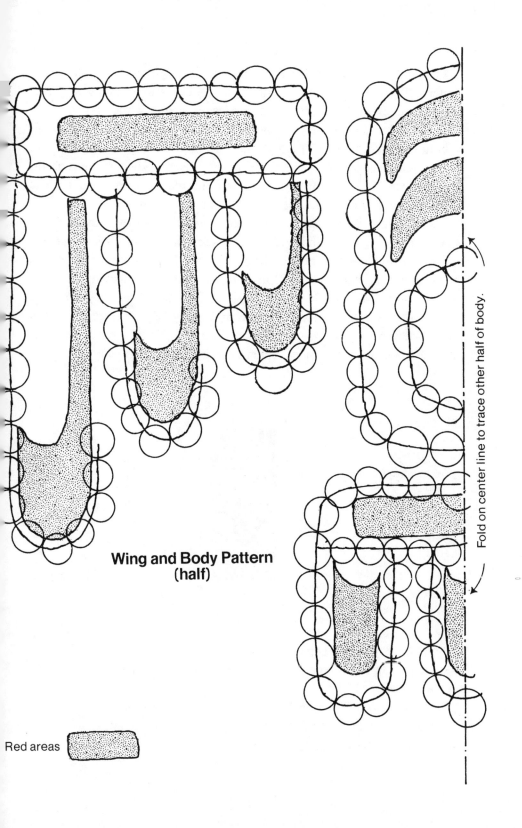

Wing and Body Pattern
(half)

Fold on center line to trace other half of body.

Red areas

On lightweight tissue, trace the button design only, from the paper pattern. Position the button pattern using the red areas as a guide. Pin the edges of the button pattern. Using strong white thread, start sewing the buttons on, sewing right through the paper. Sew up through a button, make a single stitch in back to hold it, go over to the next button and sew up through the back and secure. Sew the buttons on in rows, sewing once through each button. Place the buttons so that they form a complete outline as shown in the pattern.

Using black thread, sew on the button for the eye over the red eye shape (Fig. 3). When the bird is complete, tear off the tissue pattern.

To assemble the bag, turn under and baste ¼" all around edge of the black material. Pin the black piece to the red piece, leaving an even margin of red about 1¾" on each long side and 3¾" on each end. Sew the black piece to the red piece by hand, using an appliqué stitch (Fig. 4). If you have enough buttons you could add a border of buttons at the edge of the black material, but it's not necessary.

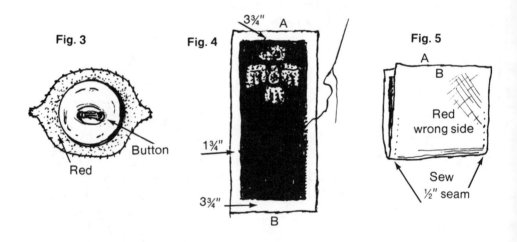

Fold up edge B to edge A, with the design inside (Fig. 5). Pin or baste side seams. Sew the sides together by machine, making ½" seam on each side.

Turn top down 2" on each end and hem. (See Fig. 8).

To make a handle, fold one side of the black strip under ½", pin and sew it by hand to the red strip ¾" in from edge, (Fig. 6). Fold the other side of the black strip under ½", fold red strip around so red edges butt each other. Pin along the edge. Sew on the other side of black strip by hand so stitches do not show. This makes a handle 2½" wide, with ½" red showing on each side of the black (Fig. 7).

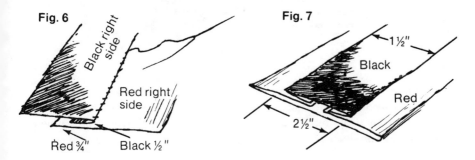

Fig. 6 Black right side
Red right/side
Red ¾" Black ½"

Fig. 7
1½"
Black
Red
2½"

To attach the handle to the bag, turn the bag wrong side out. Sew by hand attaching handle firmly to the center point, 2" down the inside the bag (Fig. 8), turning the raw ends of the handle under. Turn the bag right side out. Sew the handle to top the edge of bag (Fig. 9) and the tote bag is complete.

You may become so fond of this bold bird you'd prefer to frame it or make a wall hanging. He'd make a colorful decoration. Work him on a 12" x 13" black panel. Mount on a 15" x 16" long panel of red felt. Fold 1" of the red felt over at the top and bottom and sew to make a channel at each end. Slip rods through the channel and hang.

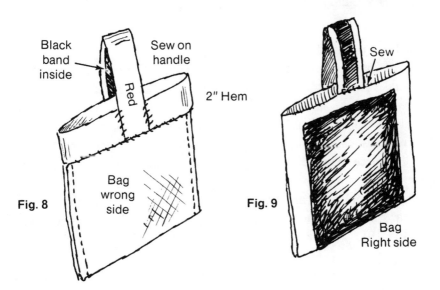

Black band inside
Sew on handle
Red
2" Hem
Bag wrong side
Fig. 8

Sew
Fig. 9
Bag Right side

149

Leather Bag

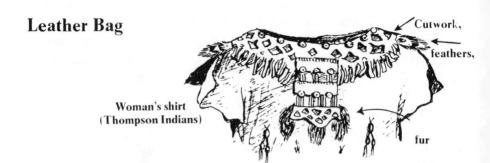

Cutwork,
feathers,

Woman's shirt
(Thompson Indians)

fur

Inspiration for a contemporary shoulder bag came from the leather cutwork on the neck of a woman's dress of a tribe that lived in the Northern Rockies. On this dress intricate cutwork contrasted with trims of feathers, fur, and feather-quills.

MATERIALS

Piece of medium weight suede leather, about 20" x 36" (size and shapes of hides vary); scrap of contrasting color suede about 8½" x 9" (or felt); for pattern, lightweight paper and brown wrapping paper; colored pencil (light color); rubber cement and fabric glue; 2 metal or wooden rings about 1¾" or 2" diameter; mat knife; polyester wrapped thread to match bag color; masking tape; stapler (optional).

For hints on handling leather see page 83.

For the pattern for the bag, see page 156. Enlarge small squares to 1" or make your own drawing, using the dimensions given and counting squares. Draw the final pattern on heavy wrapping paper. Just be sure to measure from the center points so both sides of the gusset are even. The fringe is cut of the same piece as the gusset; therefore allow a 2" x 9" piece beyond the solid area that folds over (see pattern). Gusset pattern should be 25½" in length.

For the shoulder strap, draw a strip 1½" x 36". Using the pattern, draw tabs and slots at both ends of this strip. For bag back-and-flap, draw the 19½" shape on a fold of thin paper. Cut out and open to get the complete pattern for back-and-flap. Draw the opened shape on brown paper.

For the front of the bag, cut a folded paper shape 4¼" x 10" (see pattern). Transfer the opened front shape to the brown paper. Cut out all the heavy paper shapes.

Select a flap lining. It should make a sharp contrast to the color of leather for the bag as it will show through the cutwork. Lining can be another material (such as fake fur, felt, chamois, or heavy fabric) if finding a leather piece is a problem.

For a pattern for the lining, cut a shape the exact size of the flap area if you have a large enough piece of contrasting leather or are using material. If you are using only a small scrap, make a pattern of the lower 3½" of the edge of the flap to fit behind the cut-work area. Cut a paper pattern. Using the pattern, cut the flap lining.

(If you still prefer a leather lining but can't find a scrap to use, a good substitute is a pair of suede leather elbow patches, available in notions. Lay the patches over the flap patterns (Fig. 1) and trim the patches to size—no lining pattern is needed.)

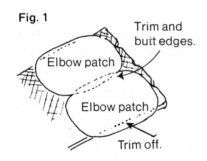

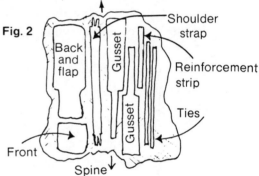

On page 155 is pattern for half of the cutwork area, actual size. Trace on folded lightweight paper, draw the other half, open it for the cutwork pattern.

To place the bag pattern on the leather for cutting, examine the leather piece. The thickness of leather varies, being thinner near edges. Often, since this is a natural material, there are flaws to avoid. Plan the shoulder strap and gussets for the heavier areas, if possible. All pieces should be placed parallel with the direction of the spine of the animal. Fig. 2 is one suggested placing.

Tape the patterns in place. With chalk or light colored pencil, draw around the paper, making an outline on the leather. Use a yardstick for the long straight lines

Most suede leathers can be cut with scissors. If the piece you are using is too heavy, place the leather on a firm cutting surface (heavy glass is good) and cut it with a mat knife.

Cut 8 pieces out of the leather: the back-and-flap piece, the front, two gussets, and a strap. Cut a 1" x 14" strip to reinforce the top edge of the bag. Cut two ⅜" x 14" strips for ties. With a knife, cut slits in the gussets and ends of the shoulder strap (Fig. 3). Do not cut the fringe, yet.

Lay the cutwork pattern on the flap, aligning the bottom edges. Tape the pattern in place and cut with mat knife working on a cutting surface. Heavy glass is best as a cutting surface because it gives the cleanest cut, but a wooden cutting board or heavy cardboard will do. Cut the openwork design carefully cutting through the pattern.

To assemble and sew the bag, you will have to use a long stitch on the sewing machine and a heavy duty needle. Try stitching on some scrap pieces first, since the tension will probably need adjusting. The stitching will be on the right side of the bag.

Lay the wide ends of the gussets together and tape to hold. Sew a ⅜" seam across ends. Open seam, brush rubber cement on both surfaces and allow to dry (Fig. 4). Then glue the seam flat (or use fabric glue).

Place the front of the bag along the edge of gusset, lining up the center front with the gusset seam. Tape together. Tape the corners to hold while sewing, or pieces can be held in place by stapling along the very outside edges (which will be trimmed later). Sew bag front to gussets (Fig. 5). Starting at center front over gusset seam, make ⅜"

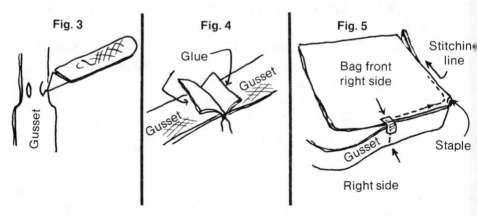

Fig. 3

Fig. 4

Fig. 5

Gusset

Glue

Gusset

Gusset

Bag front right side

Stitching line

Gusset

Staple

Right side

seam easing gusset around corner. At top end leave extra thread and cut off. Tie thread ends securely and trim. Sew up other side of front. Sew back of bag to the gussets in the same manner (Fig. 6).

Glue a reinforcement strip around the inside top front and sides (Fig. 7) with fabric glue.

Bag front right side

Fig. 6

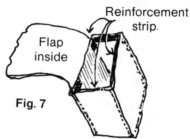

Reinforcement strip.

Flap inside

Fig. 7

Remove the tape (or staples). Open seams slightly along bag sides. Add rubber cement. When dry, stick seams together (Fig. 8). Trim evenly about ¼" beyond stitching.

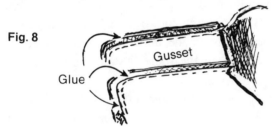

Fig. 8

Gusset

Glue

To finish, open the flap and lay bag flat. Tape the lining in position at top. Fold back the lower portion of the lining, exposing the cutwork (Fig. 9). Spread fabric glue sparingly on the wrong side of the flap around the cutwork design. Press the flap lining down and smooth. Check the cutwork from the front, and make sure suede is smooth. Remove any excess glue with wet rag. Allow to dry.

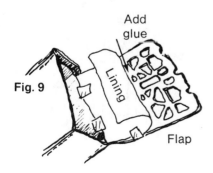

Add glue

Lining

Fig. 9

Flap

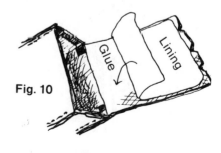

Glue

Lining

Fig. 10

153

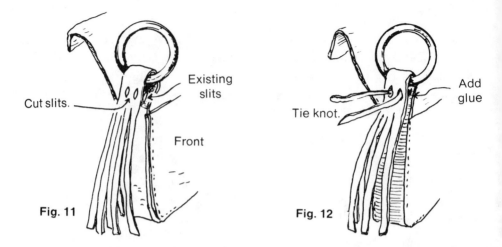

Cut slits. — Existing slits

Front

Fig. 11

Tie knot. — Add glue

Fig. 12

If the lining covers all the way up the flap, lift and brush rubber cement onto both surfaces and glue together (Fig. 10).

For the fringe on the gusset, lay the bag flat. Cut the fringe with a knife, allowing 1¾" uncut area above the top edge of bag. After cutting the fringe, fold the gusset around a ring (Fig. 11) and mark where the slits of the gussets match fold-over. Cut two slits in the fold-over area. Add rubber cement to the underside of fold-over area, and glue closed. Slide a tie through the four slits and knot (Fig. 12). Repeat on other side.

To attach the shoulder strap, put one end through the ring working from the outside in, then bring the two sections of the end through the slits (Fig. 13). Tie securely (Fig. 14). Repeat on the other ring. The bag is complete.

Fig. 13 Strap right side

Fig. 14

Tie

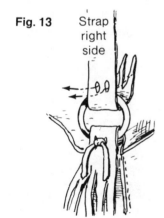

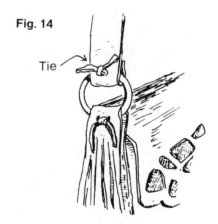

With this basic pattern you can make endless variations. The seaming can be done so it is on the inside when complete.

Instead of cutwork, you can make the flap solid and add decorations on flap, using whichever craft most delights you. Attach a copper tooled piece, or dangle some beads or shells, or fringe the edge of the flap, or add your own put-ons. At sides, instead of fringe—tie on fur tails (see p. 221 for sources).

PATTERN FOR CUTWORK OF FLAP

Place on fold of paper.

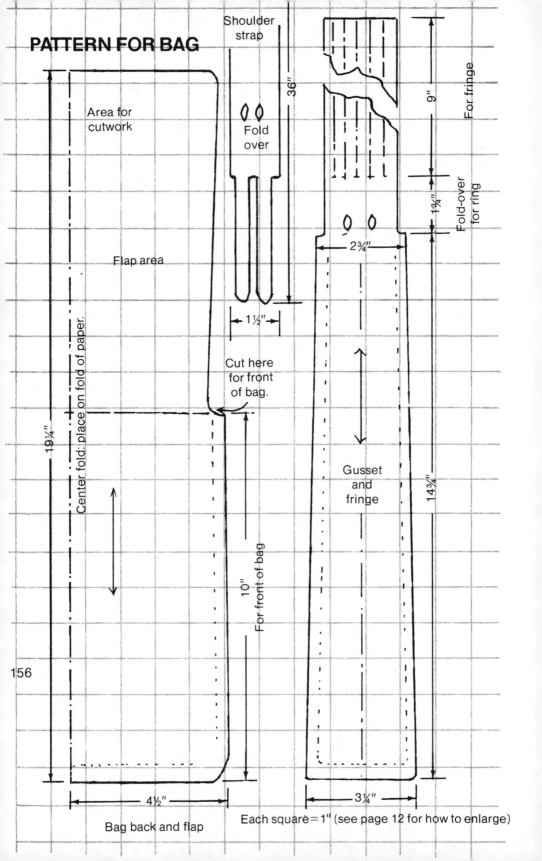

PATTERN FOR BAG

Shoulder strap

Area for cutwork

Fold over

For fringe

36"

9"

1¾"

Fold-over for ring

Flap area

2¾"

Center fold: place on fold of paper.

19¼"

Cut here for front of bag.

Gusset and fringe

14¾"

10"

For front of bag

156

4½"

3¼"

Bag back and flap

Each square = 1" (see page 12 for how to enlarge)

Quiver Muff

Do your hands get cold quickly? A quiver muff may be the answer. The Plains Indians used quivers of buffalo fur, laced at the bottom and open at the top. When the bitter winter weather struck during a hunting trip, and the arrows were gone, they could unlace the bottom of the quiver and thrust in their hands. A muff, as such, was unknown to the Indians, but these fur quivers served as a similarly pleasant source of warmth.

A quiver-muff can be a practical accessory for cold winters, even in this super-heated era.

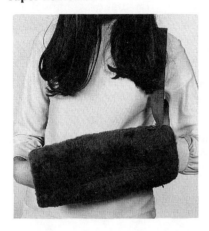

MATERIALS
20" x 30" piece of brown fake fur (or a bright color if preferred); for lining: 13½" x 16½" piece of white fake fur (or compatible color); 12½" x 14¼" lightweight cardboard, such as poster board. Leather strip 2" x 40"; for drawstring, leather thong 38"; for lacing, two 12" pieces of thong; 12" x 14" cotton sheet padding (or art foam); fabric glue; white glue.

For understructure of muff, cut a piece of cardboard 12½" x 14¼". Make sure that the grain of the cardboard curves with the 14¼" dimension (Fig. 1). Cut a piece of brown fur 20" x 30"; a piece of white fur 13¼" x 16½".

Begin by sewing one end. Put the right sides of the two fur pieces facing each other, centering the white on the brown, and aligning the bottom edge with one edge of the brown. Machine-sew the ends together making a ⅝" seam (Fig. 2).

Fig. 1

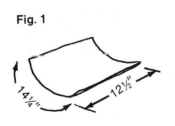

14¼" 12½"

Fig. 2

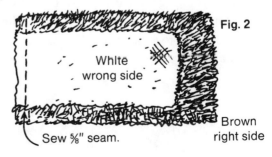

White
wrong side

Sew ⅝" seam.

Brown
right side

Fig. 3

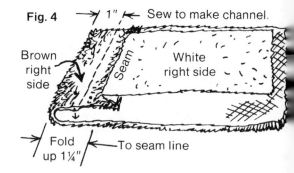

Fig. 4 → 1″ ← Sew to make channel.

Brown
right
side

Seam

White
right side

Fold for
channel edge.

White
wrong side

Fold
up 1¼″ ←— To seam line

Open fabric flat (Fig. 3), wrong side up. To make a channel for the drawstring, fold white fur over so that 1¼″ of brown fur shows (Fig. 4). Stitch 1″ from outside fold.

To assemble: Slip cardboard between furs, 3½″ from unstitched upper edge, even with white fur on one side, ¾″ of cardboard protruding from under white fur on other side (Fig. 5). Put dabs of fabric glue on upper side of cardboard and glue *white* fur to the cardboard. Brown fur must remain loose at this point. Allow glue to dry.

Open and fold brown fur back. Draw a line ¾″ from edge on unglued side of cardboard which is flush with white fur.

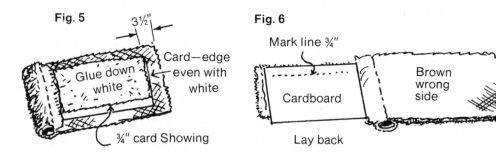

Fig. 5 3½″

Glue down white

Card—edge
even with
white

¾″ card Showing

Fig. 6

Mark line ¾″

Cardboard

Brown
wrong
side

Lay back

With brown fur hanging loose from end (Fig. 7), curve the cardboard around gently to form muff into its round shape. Overlap ¾″, aligning edge of cardboard with pencil line just drawn. Glue cardboard edge overlap together using the white glue. Hold ends with clip clothespins and put a weight inside to keep in the cylindrical shape while glue dries.

On card (underside) line drawn ¾″ from edge

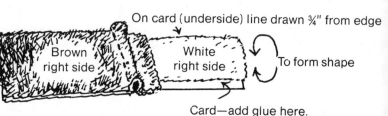

Fig. 7

Brown
right side

White
right side

To form shape

Card—add glue here.

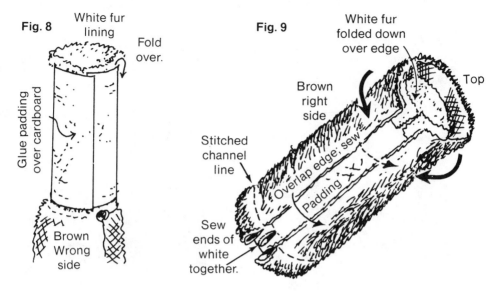

Fig. 8

White fur lining

Fold over.

Glue padding over cardboard

Brown Wrong side

Fig. 9

White fur folded down over edge

Brown right side

Top

Stitched channel line

Overlap edge; sew

Padding

Sew ends of white together.

For extra body and softness pad the muff with cotton padding or foam sheet. Glue on a piece of padding 12″ x 14″ applying fabric glue in dabs. Hold in place with rubber bands, and, when dry, remove them.

Now sew furs in place. Fold white fur down over edge of cardboard at top and glue in place with fabric glue. Fold brown fur up and around and over the padding. At bottom, sew seam in white fur where it is open below cardboard (Fig. 9). Cut the second opening for the drawstring in the brown fur channel half-way across the length of the channel. Reinforce edges of these small openings with firm stitches so it won't pull apart.

To sew brown fur around muff, overlap edges of fur along open side. Sew closed around muff, completely covering the cylinder shape in brown.

At top, fold brown inside and adjust fold-in against white fur lining that is now folded over the cardboard (Fig. 11 cross section). White

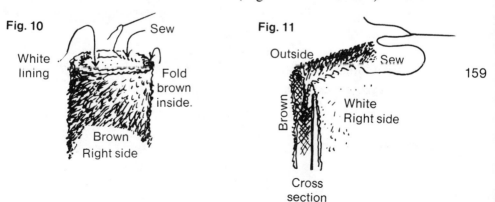

Fig. 10

Sew

White lining

Fold brown inside.

Brown Right side

Fig. 11

Outside

Sew

Brown

White Right side

Cross section

159

should come against brown, about ½″ below fold edge of brown. Fold inside less or more as necessary to make even. Pin. Then stitch the two furs together by hand (Fig. 10).

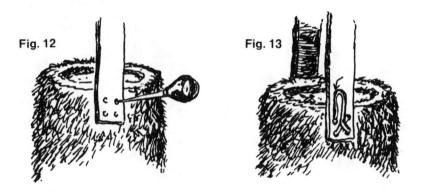

Fig. 12   Fig. 13

To complete bottom, thread in the thong drawstring (see page 85 for making drawstring). When completed, pull on both loops. They should draw the bottom closed.

To attach leather strap for carrying, punch four holes in each end of the leather strap. Strap will be positioned near top. Attach strap to each side (Fig. 12). Using an awl, make a hole through muff and push thong through holes in strap and muff to lace strap to bag. Push back through and out again making sort of an X (Fig. 13). Tie and glue ends of thong inside. Muff is complete.

To suit your mood or budget a variety of fabrics or trims could be substituted. Felt, tapestry fabric or any sturdy material could be used for the outside, with fur lining. For special elegance use real fur, either inside or out. Leather substitutes could be used for the strap. To make strap out of fabric, cut material 4″ wide, fold and sew up on wrong side. Turn, press. Sew to muff. Cords or plastic thongs could be used for drawstring.

This practical and original accessory is meant for unpredictable winter weather. With the drawstring closed, carry scarf, gloves, a soft hat, maybe an extra sweater. When braving the bitter breezes, put on the warm woolens you are carrying. Then untie the drawstring and use as a muff. When that bus that never seems to come is later than ever, this practical accessory may be frostbite insurance.

Bandolier Bag

Bandolier (Delaware)

Bandolier is a European term for a sash that crosses the chest. The Indians wore such sashes for ceremonial purposes and also carried pouches suspended from woven or leather bands that crossed the chest.

The edges of the pouch were often fringed or tasseled. Highly ornate beadwork or quillwork often covered both the bag and sash that passed across the chest to the opposite shoulder. Motifs were often floral, in direct beadwork style, with background fabric showing.

There is no questioning the practicability of such a bag. Inspired by this style, combine modern fabrics, decorative tapes, and wild colors to make your own bandolier bag.

MATERIALS

1½" yards of decorative embroidered braid 1" to 1½" wide (the pattern and color you choose for this braid determines colors and textures for the rest of the materials); 8½" x 24" piece of fabric for bag (tapestry, corduroy, suede, denim, fake fur — any sturdy fabric); 8½" x 24½" piece lining material (cotton, velour, or such); felt 1½" x42" color to go with braid (or suede leather strip); yarn, colors to complement braid; one large snap.

For the shoulder strap, cut the felt strip straight on one side. Cut braid to 42". Sewing by machine attach the braid to the felt, stitching close to edge of braid. Sew from top to bottom on each side (Fig. 1). Cut the other side of the felt even, so about ¼" of felt shows on either side of braid.

161

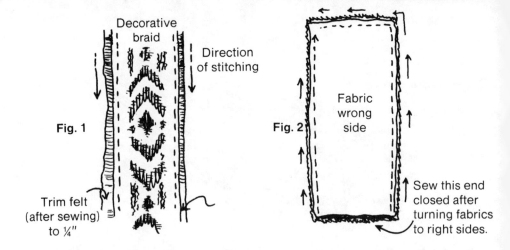

Fig. 1

Decorative braid

Direction of stitching

Trim felt (after sewing) to ¼"

Fig. 2

Fabric wrong side

Sew this end closed after turning fabrics to right sides.

For lining, place lining material and bag material right sides together. Make ½" seam. Stitch on three sides in direction of arrows (Fig. 2). Turn right side out, fold in open end ½" and sew closed by hand.

For the front of bag, fold one end up 8½" (Fig. 3). Sew the sides closed by hand, keeping stitches as invisible as possible. The flap will fold over the front of the bag at a point 10" from bottom. Place pins to mark fold on each side.

For the closure on the bag, sew on a piece of the decorative braid. Cut a piece of braid 7½" long, center it down the front of the bag, folding 1" of the braid down inside the bag. Turn under the raw edge of the braid and sew inside. Sew the braid to the front of the bag, sewing along both sides for 5½", leaving the last 1" loose. Sew across the braid 1" above end (Fig. 4). Ravel the threads of the braid to make a fringe out of that extra one inch.

To close, fold the top flap over. It should leave about 6" of front showing. Mark the position for the snap and sew on.

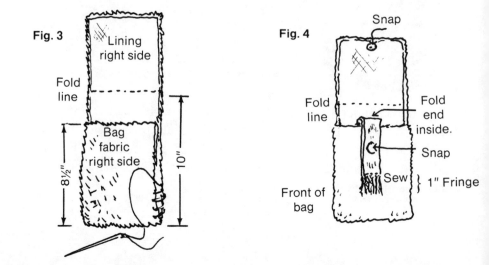

Fig. 3

Lining right side

Fold line

Bag fabric right side

8½"

10"

Fig. 4

Snap

Fold line

Fold end inside.

Snap

Sew

1" Fringe

Front of bag

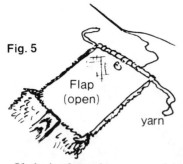

Fig. 5

Flap (open)

yarn

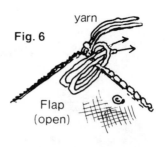

Fig. 6

yarn

Flap (open)

If desired, make a yarn fringe on the flap edge. Sew a piece of yarn across edge of flap, making stitches about ¼" apart (Fig. 5). Cut off and sew ends of yarn neatly on each side. For fringe cut about 36 pieces of yarn 7" long. Fold each piece in half. With a crochet hook, reach through under sewed yarn piece and draw the center of a 7" strand through (Fig. 6), making a loop. Pull ends through for fringe (see page 85). Repeat along the entire flap.

For the shoulder strap pin the ends to the top of the bag in the areas shown (Fig. 7). The design should face the front of bag when flap is closed. Sew straps on back of bag by hand. Sew through back only— not into lining fabric. Bandolier Bag is complete.

As with any creation, inspiration and instruction can go only so far. Your taste and imagination in the selection of pattern and color combinations determine the character of the finished product. Beading, adding beads to the fringe, tassels at the bottom of the bag—it's up to you.

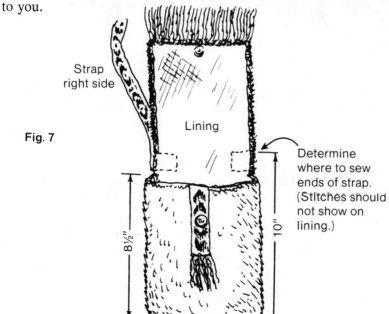

Strap right side

Lining

Fig. 7

Determine where to sew ends of strap. (Stitches should not show on lining.)

8½"

10"

ꟿFor the ꟿHead

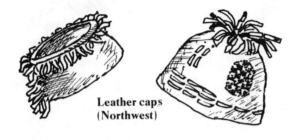

Leather caps
(Northwest)

Indians of the Northwest had practical little caps or hats made of leather. The caps sketched here, made by Indians of the Northwest, are now in a museum.

This style is just as delightful today as it was then and can be readily duplicated.

MATERIALS

Brown suede leather, two pieces about 9" x 14"; scraps of brown felt; two dozen pony beads (white and orange or colors of your choice); other beads as desired for decoration; fabric or white glue; old fabric (for pattern); embroidery hoop.

The leather you use should be soft and flexible. If you can't find suede, use chamois which is easily available in all hardware and variety stores. Two small pieces or one large one will probably be sufficiently large for the project.

For a pattern, enlarge the shape on page 166 on a folded piece of paper. Trace on other side. Open to get the shape shown (Fig. 1). This is half the hat. The lines for cutting in the fringes need not be traced. They are only a guide to show you where to cut (when you get to that step). The fringe can be any length that will fit on your leather piece. If some parts are shorter, it won't hurt.

If you are using chamois, mix brown liquid dye as directed and dip chamois in dye. Leave until it acquires a desired depth of color. Rinse

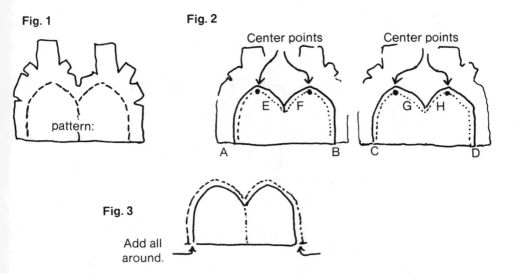

Fig. 1

pattern:

Fig. 2

Center points

Center points

E F

G H

A

B

C

D

Fig. 3

Add all around.

and dry. Stretch and shape chamois flat as it dries. Kneading it in your hands will soften and shape it.

Before cutting the leather, make a pattern of old fabric to check the fit. Using the paper pattern cut out two pieces of old fabric. Pin or baste the seams together.

The hat is shaped by sewing the seams as follows (Fig. 2). Sew E to F and G to H. Sew A and D together up to the center point on the top of that side. Then sew B to C up to the center point on the other side. Be sure not to catch in the fringe edges as you sew. The seams are on the right side—later they will make the fringe.

Try on the fabric hat. If it is too tight, make the pattern slightly larger (Fig. 3). Cut another piece of old fabric and repeat to make sure of the size. If the hat is too loose, make the seams deeper.

When you are satisfied with the fit, take out the seams. Using the fabric as a pattern, cut the shapes out of leather (or chamois). Sew the seams in leather on the machine, using a long stitch. Assemble the hat as described in Fig. 2.

To finish the bottom edge, turn the edge inside ⅛" and glue with fabric glue (or rubber cement).

165

With the pattern (page 166) as a guide, cut in the fringes. Cut almost to the seam, being very careful not to cut into stitching. Strips should be about ¼" wide.

CAP PATTERN

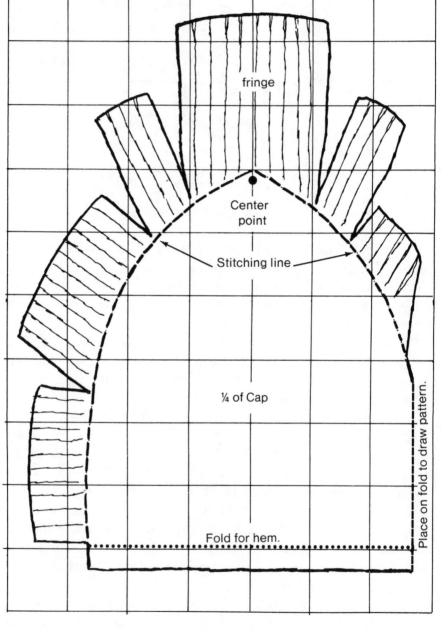

fringe

Center point

Stitching line

¼ of Cap

Place on fold to draw pattern.

Fold for hem.

166

Each square = 1″ (see page 12 for how to enlarge)

Fig. 4

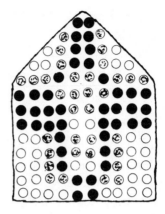

Fig. 5

Sew a beaded design along the edge (Fig. 4) by sewing in and out of the leather, using the direct beading method. Use a variety of bead shapes and sizes.

For beaded panels, trace the shape shown in Fig. 5. Draw four of these shapes on the brown felt. Stretch on an embroidery hoop and work one panel at a time. Apply beads, seed or "real," using the two needles method (see page 30). When the beading is complete on a motif, tie the ends firmly. Cut out the shape as closely as possible to the outside beads without cutting the beading threads. Bead the other three shapes as above, and glue the beaded motifs to the hat, centering one motif in each panel.

To add beads to the fringe, fold a piece of fringe in half and slip a pony bead over. As the fold opens, the bead will be held in place. If the bead tends to slide, add a dab of glue with a toothpick and slip the bead over the glue. Repeat, placing beads in a random pattern throughout the fringe until you have enough to make it look attractive.

Of course, this is only a basic idea. You can make all sorts of variations to suit your whims.

If expense is a consideration, the hat could be made of felt instead of leather; the beads could be dyed tubettini.

Colors can be "now" rather than traditional. Dye or buy suede or chamois in purple, pink or orange. Add beads of similarly brilliant colors. Make color even or tie dye.

167

Another idea: Buy white or a very light color suede or use the natural color of the chamois. Omit the beading. With felt markers draw fun designs all over and color them in with wild colors: Take it from here with your own ideas.

The Bag

Turn the hat upside down and you have the start of a drawstring bag. Add 8" to the pattern (Fig. 6). Cut two felt or leather pieces (four panels), and proceed to assemble them as for the hat. Turn down 1½" hem at top. Sew or glue along the edge, leaving an opening for a channel (Fig. 7). Turn right side out. For drawstrings, thread two 30" thongs or cords through the top hem (see page 85). Cut a fringe and bead it in any spots desired.

Or it could be a tiny pouch to hang from your belt. Use only two panels of the hat size pattern. Sew up (Fig. 8) around the edges. Cut a fringe and bead. Fold the top edge inside 1". Sew, or glue about ¼", leaving a channel. Add a drawstring. Hang from a belt by the drawstring.

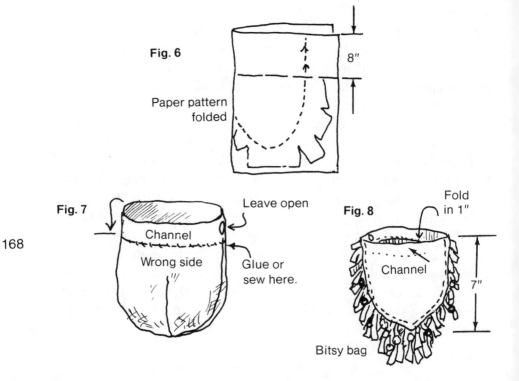

Fig. 6

Paper pattern folded

8"

Fig. 7

Leave open

Channel

Wrong side

Glue or sew here.

Fig. 8

Fold in 1"

Channel

7"

Bitsy bag

Headbands

Headbands or brow bands have again come into fashion in recent times. Few tribes wore a decorative band of this type. Indians of the far West wore bands on their heads to relieve the pressure from burden baskets. Ceremonial feathers were sometimes held in place by a brow band. The highly decorative beaded band at the front of the familiar war bonnet may have inspired today's fad.

Many ideas in this book can be adapted for making headbands. Woven, tied or sewed, the ideas for belts, sashes, necklaces can be adapted. Decorative braid sewn to felt (page 162) makes a quick colorful band.

Once you master your loom, you can create hand beaded or woven bands. Bead the whole headband or bead about 8" and attach beading to a ribbon backing. Using a 1½"- or 2"-wide ribbon for a base, all sorts of decorations can be added.

A band of felt pieces can be very snappy. Here is one inspired by the painted and woven designs of the Northwest Indians. Since their food supply was primarily fish, fish motifs naturally appeared in much of their art.

MATERIALS

1½" x 20" strip of red felt; small scraps of black, white, blue, orange, light green felt; seed beads: a few white, yellow, two black; fabric glue.

The designs will be cut of felt, the smaller shapes will be layered on top of the larger shapes.

For patterns of the center unit trace motifs on paper (Fig. 1). Cut of felt. Place three pieces on top of each other to create the design (Fig. 2).

169

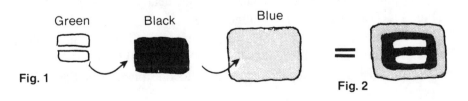

Green   Black   Blue   =

Fig. 1   Fig. 2

For the whale pattern, (Fig. 3), trace the outline on paper. Cut two shapes of black felt. Trace the smaller shapes on paper. With small sharp scissors, cut fins, backbone spots, mouth, eye and tail spots out of felt as shown. Cut two of each. One set will be reversed so that the two fish will face the motif in the center.

Stack all the pieces together (the two fish facing each other). Make

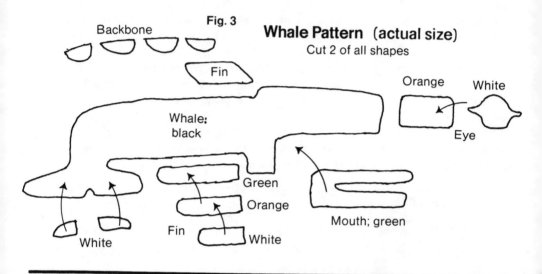

Fig. 3

Whale Pattern (actual size)
Cut 2 of all shapes

Backbone

Fin

Whale: black

Orange   White

Eye

Green

Orange

Mouth; green

Fin   White

White

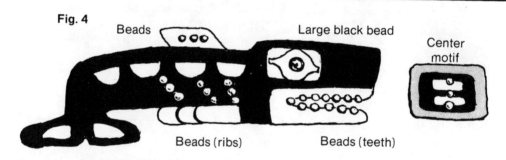

Fig. 4

Beads

Large black bead

Center motif

Beads (ribs)   Beads (teeth)

certain that all the pieces fit over each other neatly to create the design (Fig. 4). Trim if necessary to align edges.

To assemble, lay the two fish and the center motif on the band. They should occupy about 11″ overall. Space them so that the band looks attractive. Using a toothpick, apply glue to one piece at a time. Glue down, starting with smallest spots. Glue all the pieces to large piece, then glue the large piece to the band. Weight with a heavy book and let set until dry.

To complete, sew on seed beads, going through only the upper layers of felt (if possible) so that the back will be smooth. Put in a row of white teeth on each whale, yellow or green beads for the ribs, three colored beads in the upper fin (Fig. 4). Sew three beads in the center design.

Try on the headband to get the proper size, then pin where the ends overlap. Sew ends together.

If this is to be a choker, use an 1¼" x 11" piece of felt, round the corners, and apply the design. Sew narrow ribbon or cord to the ends of the felt to tie in back. This whale pattern could be used for decoration on pocket flaps, belts or other accessories.

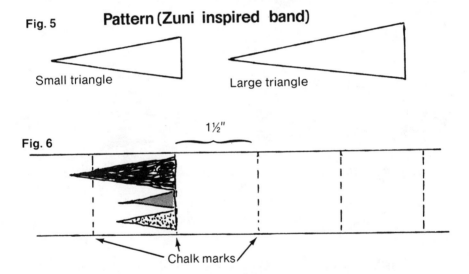

Fig. 5   **Pattern (Zuni inspired band)**

Small triangle   Large triangle

1½"

Fig. 6

Chalk marks

Another felt design that is fun and can use up all sorts of felt scraps is this arrangement of triangles inspired by Zuni woven patterns. Cut a black felt headband 1½" x 20".

For the pattern, trace the two triangle shapes shown on paper (Fig. 5). Using the paper pattern, cut triangles out of bright colored felts, using as many colors as possible. Cut about 8 long triangles, 28 small ones. If you need more, cut them as needed.

171

With white chalk, mark vertical lines across the black felt 1½"
apart (Fig. 6). Starting at the left, place one large triangle at the top
of row and two small triangles below. Line up the bases of triangles
with the white chalk guide lines.

Skip a space and place two small triangles with large triangle at
bottom, skip a row and repeat (Fig. 7). After going all across the band
in this manner, go back and put two small triangles in each of the areas
skipped (Fig. 8). After all the triangles are laid in position, transpose
some triangles, if necessary, to get as lively a color ararngement as
possible.

When satisfied with arrangement of colors, pick up one triangle at a
time, put glue on the back and replace the triangle in the position
planned. Go on to the next one. Glue triangles along the entire strip.
Don't make it look too geometric—a little variation gives it a more
interesting look. Finish the band as before.

Fig. 7

| Skip | 2 small | Skip | 1 large |
| space | 1 large | space | 2 small |

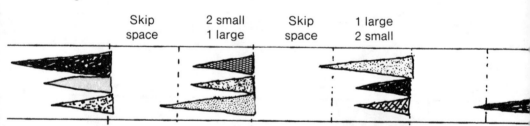

Fig. 8

Add 2 small   Add 2 small
(upper area)   (lower area)

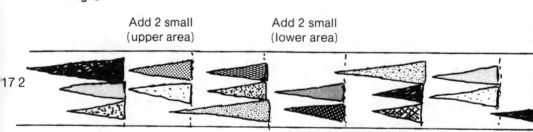

Footwear

"Moccasin" is an Algonquin word which now generally applies to most all Indian-type leather foot coverings. There were countless variations of this footgear throughout the continent. On the following page are some sketches to show a few of the typical shapings with some of the basic seam constructions.

The simplest design was made of one piece of leather with the center seam over the toe (see Row 1). More familiar, however, is the moccasin constructed with side and sole of one piece, and a center insert over the toe (Row 2).

The Plains Indians sometimes cut the leather to form a seam at the side near the sole (see Row 3). This made shapes for the right and left feet, a comfortable idea developed long before the Europeans thought of it.

Other variations included different combinations of seams and inserts. Tongues, in many shapes, were added or shaped from the same pieces as the basic moccasin. Cuffs were sometimes narrow, others were huge and could be pulled up around the ankles.

Foot protection in the rocky, cactus-filled terrain of the Southwest needed very sturdy soles. Here heavy leather was soaked and shaped to give depth to the sole. Soft uppers were wrapped and sewn to the sole (Row 5). Sometimes tops were high, giving the appearance of a boot. In some tribes, women's boots wound around the legs up to the knee, using up a whole deer skin for one pair.

Of course, in the snow and ice of the Far North, tall fur boots were needed for protection. The Eskimos developed, therefore, the practical and well shaped "Mukluk."

The Indians often added decorations to their moccasins. The Plains Indians, especially, made splendid decorations on their moccasins.

Some of the finest quill and beadwork ornamented Indian footwear. Usually decorative work was done before assembling the moccasin. Pieces of beadwork often covered seams along toes and heels. The upper toe areas lent themselves to a variety of decorations. Below are a few typical designs. Beadwork or other sewn-on ornamentation sometimes edged the cuffs. In some areas, cuffs were fringed, sometimes the tongue or heel had a fringe.

Where climate and terrain was favorable, no foot covering was necessary or used. Sandals provided sole protection in warm climates. Made of leather or woven of sturdy natural fibers, sandals were worn mostly in the far West and Southwest.

173

Quill
(Mandan)

Bead, crooked nose
design
(Blackfoot)

Bead
(Dakota)

Quill
(Cheyenne)

Bead
(Seneca)

FOOTWEAR

	LEATHER PARTS	ASSEMBLED	VARIATIONS
EASTERN	Toe seam / Sole / seam / Heel	One piece; center seam	Gathered or puckered toe
	Sole / Heel / Insert	Round insert, plus cuff	Narrow insert; no cuff
WESTERN	Top / Fold / Sole / Heel	Often had added cuff	Boot top sewn on
	Tongue / Top / Sole / Heel		Fringes, toe more pointed
SOUTHWESTERN	Flap / Top / Toe / Shaped sole		At various periods, styles changed in various areas. This is only a brief chart of basic constructions.

174

Mock Moccasins

Since there are many moccasin kits available in craft and supply places it's more fun to create the whimsical decorations. The kits vary in price, depending on the quality of the leather used and how carefully they are designed to fit. There are also patterns for sale permitting you to choose your own leather, if you prefer.

MATERIALS: Moccasin kit; type with rounded insert; (or pattern and necessary materials); trim materials (your choice).

Plan what sort of trim you will put on your moccasin. In most cases it is easier to attach beads or other decoration before lacing up the moccasin pieces. Trims that hide joinings and lacings must be attached after assembly.

Assemble moccasins according to directions on the kit. (Or make them using your own pattern.) Then personalize it. There are many ways, here are a few suggestions:

1. Fur trim. Using a leather cuff for a pattern, cut a cuff out of fake fur. If you want furry linings for your moccasins measure the depth and cut the cuff wider to fit down inside. Lace on the fur piece instead of the leather cuff. Use an awl to punch holes through the fur for a lace to pass through. Lace the moccasin together. Cut a fur piece slightly larger than the toe section. Glue on to the top of the moccasin, hiding the toe lacings. Tie the lace in front through the fur (Fig. 1).

2. Upholstery trims can add a bright note. Buy yarn edging, ball fringe or a sturdy decorative pattern edging that will make a lively combination with the leather color. Glue the edging onto the cuff. Glue and/or sew around and over the front lacing seam (or next to seam). Cut some fringe, make a tassel, sew to ties (Fig. 2) or use a ball from the ball fringe to decorate the tie.

3. Of course, beadwork makes moccasins look authentic if that is what you prefer. Sew on loom beading or bead a motif onto the leather. Don't try to sew *through* the leathers, go through only the upper layers. An easier method is to bead a design on felt (see page 29) and then glue this to the leather (Fig. 3).

4. Add significant motifs. The many stick-on or sew-on motifs available today are great for moccasin decorating. Make it hearts and flowers

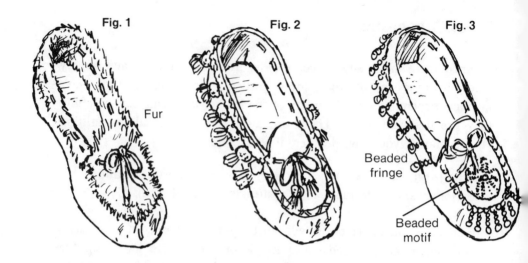

Fig. 1 — Fur

Fig. 2

Fig. 3 — Beaded fringe — Beaded motif

or whatever. Glue or sew on these motifs in any wild arrangement you choose. Add a decorative ribbon or braid to cuffs (Fig. 4). Or draw designs on the leather with colorful felt tipped markers. Add a felt fringe to the cuff (Fig. 5).

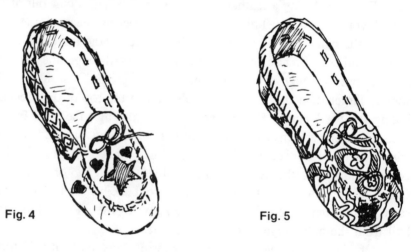

Fig. 4

Fig. 5

176

5. Instead of fringe, some tribes made hair trims. Combined with quill embroidery it gave an elegant effect (Fig. 6). Clumps of hair, (moose maybe) were tied in bundles (Fig. 7). Sometimes these bundles were banded with quill or beadwork. For others, metal was beaten thin and shaped around bundles.

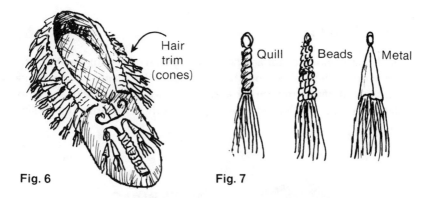

Hair trim (cones)

Quill Beads Metal

Fig. 6 Fig. 7

Using this idea, make some cone trims. For "hair," cut a strip of burlap about 1½" wide. Ravel out the threads. For cone, cut shape shown (Fig. 8) out of the side of an alminum can. Curve this shape around the tip of an awl, forming a cone. Insert a clump of the raveled threads. Add in one longer thread, doubled, to make a hanging loop (Fig. 9). Use a little glue to hold it. Complete by closing the cone around the threads, using pliers if necessary. Make as many as desired.

Sew the cone trim to a design that is beaded or glued on the toes or attach cones to ends of the laces. Sew a row along the cuff for a fringe effect if desired.

Fig. 8 Fig. 9

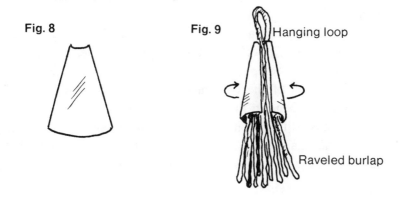

Hanging loop

Raveled burlap

These ideas should get you started. If you make up a kit and find that the moccasins fit well, it could be disassembled and used as a pattern. Make moccasins out of other leathers, add other materials, such as fake fur, tapestry, a piece of rug, etc. Crochet or needlepoint the toes and cuffs, if that is what you enjoy doing.

Even with humble kit beginnings, you can be creative.

177

Woven Sandal

The Indians would adapt any practical method of making an object to other uses whenever there was a need. You can similarly adapt a technique used for one sort of object to another use, with pleasing and practical results. This modern adaptation of basket weaving can result in a sturdy and original pair of sandals.

MATERIALS

Clothesline cord approximately ¼" in diameter (about 30 feet); two balls of wrapping twine (or jute or other flexible but sturdy cord); two ¼"-wide leather strips about 20" long; heavy, blunt, large-eyed yarn needle; glue.

The twine, interwoven around the clothesline cord, makes a sturdy sole. The wrapping twine should be durable but flexible (some may be a bit too stiff).

For a medium sized sandal, cut about 12 feet of the clothesline cord, more for a large foot. Cut off a working length of twine, about a yard, and thread it on the needle.

Fold back the end of the cord against itself about 6½" (Fig. 1). Start weaving at the bend in the cord.

The basic weave throughout is a simple figure-eight. Lay a short end of the twine against the cord, go between and over and around two cords (Fig. 1). Continue weaving between the two cord sections to

Fig. 1

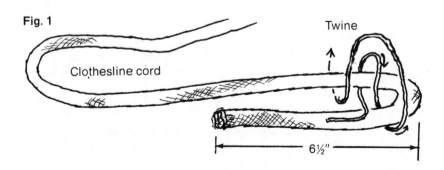

Clothesline cord

Twine

6½"

Fig. 2

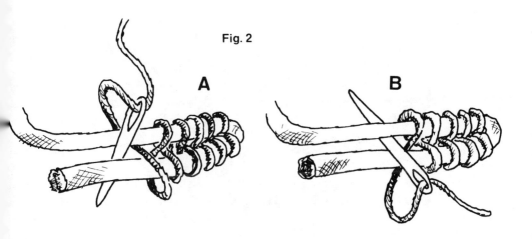

hold them securely together (Figs, 2A and B). Space the cord loops about ⅛″ apart. The spaces in between the twine will be filled in as you work the next row around.

On reaching the end of the fold, bend the next section of cord around, and lay it next to the part already worked (Fig. 3). Continue the figure-eight. The weave this time goes: one loop of twine around the new strand of cord, the other loop of twine around previously wound cord sections—go between each loop of twine on the cord. This should fill the previously woven row solidly so that no clothesline cord shows (Fig. 4). If you see that some cord shows at the points where it

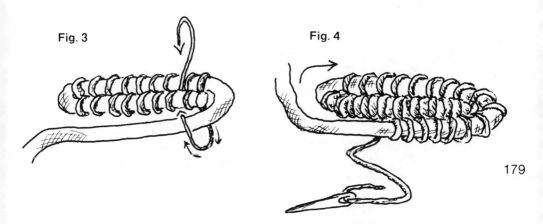

Fig. 3

Fig. 4

Note: These are simplified diagrams. There will be many more stitches on the actual piece.

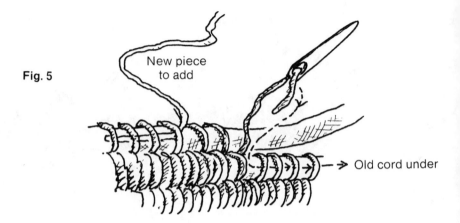

Fig. 5

New piece
to add

Old cord under

bends, wrap a few turns of twine around the cord to hide it, then continue.

To add a new piece of twine as the old one begins to run short, lay the end of a new twine piece under the work as you weave. It will be firm by the time you need it (Fig. 5). With the needle, slide the end of the old piece of twine down under weaving and trim off.

To determine when the size of the sandal is correct, occasionally place your foot on this sole. Continue going around and around, keeping the cord flat until the desired size of sole is attained.

To make the tabs at the side, continue weaving in the same manner. Fold the cord, making three small turns as shown (Fig. 6). Do one

Fig. 6

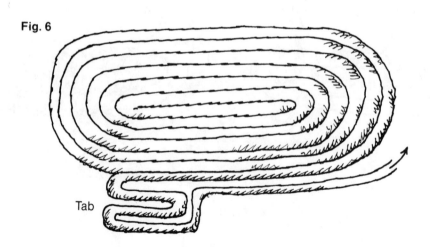

Tab

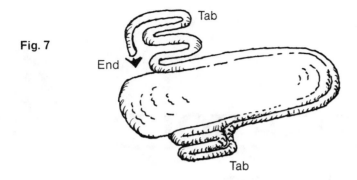

Fig. 7

Tab

End

Tab

side, work the cord around to the front and do the other side tab (Fig. 7). Cut off at the point shown (Fig. 7) and weave twine several times around end to secure. Run twine under the weaving and cut off.

To attach the thong, place your foot on the sandal to determine the spot where the leather will come between your toes. Work the leather up through the weaving at this point. If the weaving is too tight, use the tips of *closed* scissors to separate the twine enough for an opening. Bring the leather piece up through the sole and over to one side tab, through that tab then over to the other side through the tab as shown (Fig. 8). Go back down through the same hole in the sole. Try on your foot, adjust the lengths of leather in the tabs so that the sandal fits comfortably. Pull the thong out at the bottom and tie (Fig. 9). Use glue to secure the leather tie.

Repeat the entire process to make the other sandal.

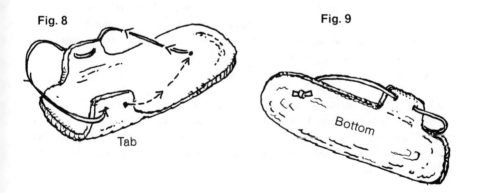

Fig. 8

Fig. 9

Tab

Bottom

181

HOUSEHOLD 4

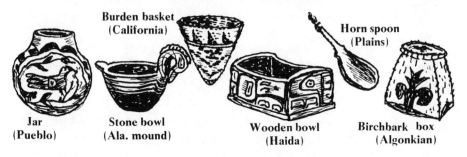

Burden basket
(California)

Horn spoon
(Plains)

Jar
(Pueblo)

Stone bowl
(Ala. mound)

Wooden bowl
(Haida)

Birchbark box
(Algonkian)

The design and degree of ornamentation of the Indians' household articles varied according to tribe. Settled groups with permanent homes lavished more work on these articles than the more migratory tribes. Baskets, spoons, bowls, jars, trays and boxes were made of various natural materials. In the Northwest, walls and posts were carved, inlaid or painted. In the Southwest, walls in certain special rooms were painted.

Indian inspired household items can also enliven your surroundings.

Walls and Floors

The rug, as we know it, is not really an Indian idea. Many tribes wove practical grass or straw type mats for the floor and for sitting. Undoubtedly old robes were also used to sit on. But most of the well-known woven rugs with elegant patterns are made for the tourist trade.

Rag Rug

This rag rug was inspired by mats made for sitting by Indians in the Northeast. The mats sometimes had fabric strips woven in with plant fibers. As garments wore out, serviceable sections were used and reused. Finally the last strips were pieced and woven into mats. This was one ancestor of the Rag Rug.

182

MATERIALS Four skeins or more of rug yarn (depending on size of rug you are making); crochet hook (K); scraps of cotton or wool fabrics.

To make a mesh for weaving-in fabric strips, crochet a mesh as described on page 104. Determine the width desired for rug, make the starting chain this size, then crochet rows until the desired length is reached. Each 70 yard skein of rug yarn will make a piece of mesh approximately 9" x 18". Figure your needs from this.

For fabric to weave through the mesh, cut or tear fabric into strips about 2½" wide and about 2" longer than width of rug. If the fabric is thin, make wider strips; if the fabric is bulky, make narrower ones. Experiment to find what is needed to fill snugly each open square of mesh. If scraps are not long enough to go across rug, sew pieces together (with sewing machine), then cut strips to size.

Fold fabric so that the fraying edges are on the inside (Figs. 1A & B). Weave the strips of fabric through the mesh you've crocheted. Use a great variety of colors and patterns to achieve an old-fashioned rag rug look. Or choose your color, make a dark band on each end and bright colors in the middle—whatever effect you desire.

To finish, fold the strip ends under and sew them on each side. Make sure no raw, ravelled edges show (Fig. 2).

Other durable discards that can make a great rug are all those old nylons and pantyhose with runs. To make the rug, crochet a mesh no more than 31" wide, but as long as desired. Cut off the toes and tops of nylons. Weave the nylons through the mesh, using two at a time. This should fill the holes, but you may need three if the nylons are sheer. You'll have to experiment to see. Crocheted mesh holes should be *densely* filled. Sew the ends firmly.

Make this rug mostly in tan tones from the mountains of discards everybody will be delighted to find a home for. Or you may wish to use colored stockings or pantihose. Nylons can also be dyed with fabric dyes. Follow the package directions for removing the tan color and dying color desired.

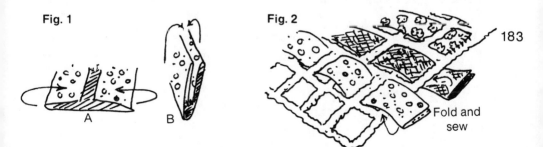

Fig. 1

A   B

Fig. 2

Fold and sew

183

A Natural Hang-Up

The Indians believed that every living thing, even trees and plants, had a spirit and soul Most people today have such a distant relationship with nature that they can never return to the quiet respect the Indian had for natural elements. The best we can do is to keep around us some reminders of natural beauty, fit that beauty into our own surroundings so it can be admired daily.

This wall hanging consists of wild grasses and reeds, woven through rough yarn. If you have woven even a small piece of fabric on the loom described in Chapter II, you can make this wall hanging.

MATERIALS

For the warp, a ball of nubby-textured yarn, brown or natural (or dye a ball of ordinary white string); for the weft, contrasting yarns (such as brown, white, hot orange); an assortment of dried material: grasses, sea grass, reeds, etc.; two 16" or 17" long reasonably straight natural sticks (or two ½" dowels); blunt yarn needle; loom (as described on page 114).

There are many kinds of dried materials that would be good for this project. Here is a partial list: thin driftwood, dried mosses, wheat, dried seaweed, reeds, dried corn husk, cattails, tiny straw flowers, feathers, silver dollar or honesty. You can no doubt think of many others. Florists, variety stores and many craft supply places sell material for dried floral arrangements. Often you can buy an assortment if you have no access to collecting your own.

184

Assemble the loom as described (pp. 115-117). If possible use natural sticks in place of the top and bottom dowels as they will remain in the final wall hanging and blend in with natural elements better. If you are using dowels for rods, stain the dowels and finish the ends before setting up the loom.

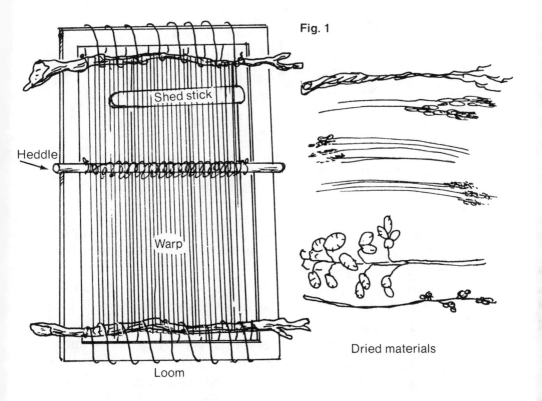

Fig. 1

Shed stick

Heddle

Warp

Loom

Dried materials

For the warp, wind the string around top and bottom rods, spacing about ⅜″ apart. Tie on to the frame with cords. Place the upper shed stick in position and attach the heddle stick (see loom instructions page 116). Now you are ready to weave (Fig. 1).

Plan your design. The yarns will contrast with the grasses and help hold the whole piece together. Most of the space should be filled with the natural elements. Many areas can be left open with the warp showing. The whole process will proceed much faster than tight weaving.

Place your dried material next to the loom and try to visualize how it will look when woven in. Plan what sequence to use (Fig. 1). Plan your sections of yarn trying to visualize texture and color needed. Make a little sketch if it will help. Plan for a variety of yarn textures and color combinations.

185

Begin weaving when you have laid out an arrangement that seems interesting. Weave about 2″ of yarn up from the bottom to secure the rod in place and give body to the hanging. With a fork, push the first few rows of yarn tightly against rod. Space the next few rows of weav-

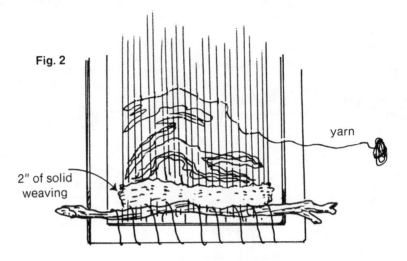

Fig. 2

2" of solid weaving

yarn

ing, shaping them with a fork, to make interesting waves or rhythms (Fig. 2). Weave some rows only part way across. There are no rules. Be free and follow your whims.

To insert grasses and other dried materials, open the shed as wide as possible. Gently slide grasses between the warp strands. Shift to the other warp shed and weave in some yarn. Make several rows to secure the material in place. If the grasses are not bulky, they can be inserted in opposite sheds, just like weft threads. Some of the more supple grasses can be shifted with the fork to form waves and patterns (Fig. 3) —it will depend on the material you use. Ends of dried material should protrude from each side—it adds to the effect.

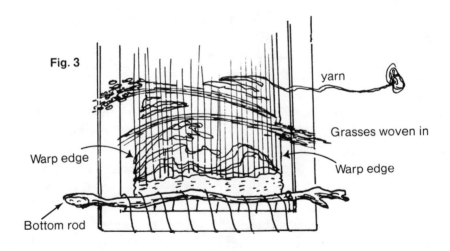

Fig. 3

yarn

Grasses woven in

Warp edge

Warp edge

Bottom rod

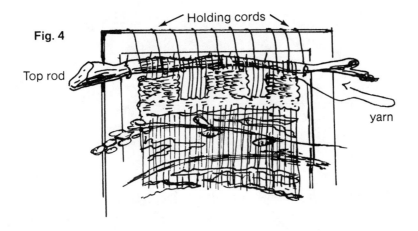

Fig. 4

Holding cords

Top rod

yarn

After inserting bulky items such as driftwood or branches, weave (by hand if necessary) sections of yarn around them to reestablish the shed, otherwise it may be hard to open the opposite shed.

As you near the top it will become more difficult to add bulky items. Put in flatter items and do more yarn weaving. About 2½" from top it will be necessary to remove the shed stick and heddle.

To complete, thread yarn on a yarn needle and hand weave (over and under), filling in the distance to the top. It's not necessary to weave all the way across. Sections could be woven part of the way for various effects (Fig. 4).

Now examine your wall hanging. Does it need more color accents? Are there too many open areas? Does it need more rhythm? With the fork, shift and push the units up and down on the warp for more movement. Thread a yarn needle with the yarn and weave in and around materials to add body or more color accents where needed. Trim some excess material at sides, but do leave 2" or 3" of interesting dried flower or seed heads sticking out.

The beauty of this type of wall hanging depends on the balance and contrasts of textures and colors. Natural elements and woven areas must complement each other. You can only judge just how much to add as you work.

187

When you are satisfied that the weaving is complete, cut the holding cords (*not* the warp). Remove the weaving from the frame, gently lifting the piece by the top and bottom rods.

Fig. 5

Tie

Tie a cord or thong on each side of the top rod (Fig. 5) and your creation is ready to be hung. Your wall color will add dimension to the hanging.

Part of the excitement of this type of weaving is that there will never be a duplicate. Let your imagination go free to find materials to add.

In addition to weaving with grasses, you can tie small things such as seeds, beads, shells, a sand dollar or dried fungus onto the weft thread as you weave. Artistic enough for a museum, personal enough for any room, these wall hangings are a tribute to nature and your artistic sense.

Felt Hanging

You can adapt whatever Indian designs you choose for wall hangings. The wall hanging shown was inspired by a decorated legging seen in a museum.

The diagram on the opposite page gives you most of the information you'll need. It's not necessary to copy it exactly. Make it in bright colors, if you like, and any size that suits the space you wish to fill. The one shown had a finished size of 12" x 16".

MATERIALS

12½" x 29" piece of tan velour or felt (or any color fabric: wool, cotton, or other sturdy fabric); scraps and pieces of black and red felt; one skein black bulky yarn; "real" beads in red, white, yellow and black (or colors preferred); four ⅜" red wooden beads (optional); 14" black rickrack, 1 package of black soutache, and, 14" red soutache braid; fabric glue; 14" hanging rod (either a ⅜" dowel or cafe curtain rod).

BUTTERFLIES IN THE SANDHILLS

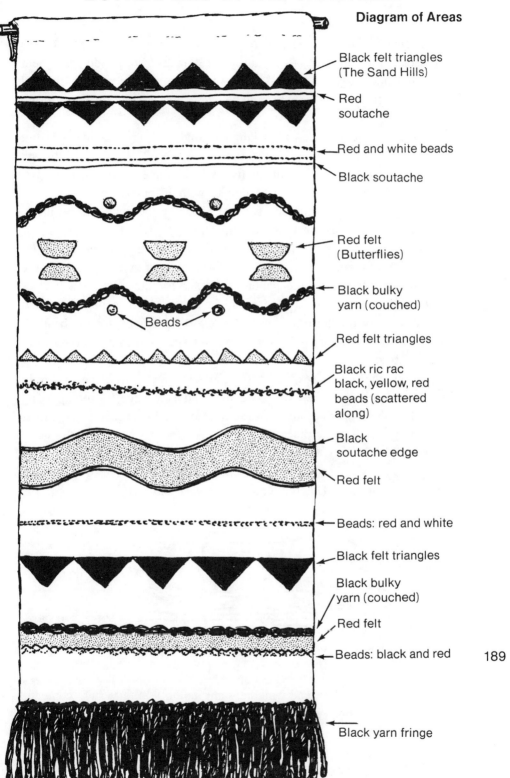

Diagram of Areas

Black felt triangles
(The Sand Hills)

Red
soutache

Red and white beads

Black soutache

Red felt
(Butterflies)

Black bulky
yarn (couched)

Beads

Red felt triangles

Black ric rac
black, yellow, red
beads (scattered
along)

Black
soutache edge

Red felt

Beads: red and white

Black felt triangles

Black bulky
yarn (couched)

Red felt

Beads: black and red

Black yarn fringe

189

On paper, plan your design to fit the fabric you plan to use. If you are using fabric instead of felt, allow ½" on each long side for a hem when finishing edges. Allow 3" on top to turn under to make a channel for the hanging rod. The hem may be as deep as desired on the bottom, but allow for it.

Figure out sizes needed for triangular shapes. They should come out even with width of fabric. For instance: on the 12" finished width, six triangles with 2" bases will fit, or five with about 2⅜" bases. For rows of smaller "sandhills," make 12 triangles with 1" bases.

Plan your rows of beads, ric rac, etc., spacing the items interestingly. For the curved areas, draw the design on paper, fold the paper in half and trace the design on the other side in order to get the curve on both sides the same. For the butterfly motif, draw one half of the butterfly on paper, fold the paper, and trace for the other side.

Draw indications of the design on the fabric. With a pencil draw a straight line for the bottom edge of the rows of triangles; for the beading lines, etc. Use a tracing wheel and transfer sheets to mark curved lines on the fabric.

Cut out the felt pieces, using the pattern paper. Glue the pieces in the position planned. Sew on soutache braid (see page 93 for applying soutache). Sew or glue on rick-rack. Cut out the curved red felt piece, glue or appliqué it in place. Edge with soutache or sew beads along the edge

The bulky yarn should be "couched" in position. This is a simple sewing technique that merely catches the yarn onto the fabric (Fig. 1).

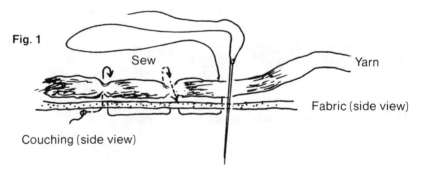

Fig. 1
Sew
Yarn
Fabric (side view)
Couching (side view)

190

With a needle and thread (in the same color as the yarn), come up from back of fabric. Place the yarn along the line of the design. Take

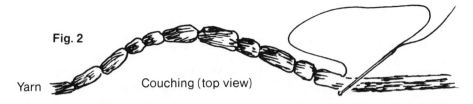

Fig. 2

Yarn   Couching (top view)

the thread around the yarn and sew back into the fabric at almost the same spot. Come up again about ¼" further along line. Go up around the yarn and back in and repeat. Do not sew into the yarn, only around it. Stitches can be farther apart on straight work, closer together for curves. For this hanging, stitches can be spaced unevenly, varying from ⅛" to ⅝", approximately (Fig. 2). Yarn should puff up slightly between each stitch.

Sew beads on by the direct method, scattering them along the rickrack. Sew straight rows of beads, alternating colors. On the bottom row, the beads can hang slightly (Fig. 3). String on 5 beads, sew into the fabric sufficiently close to the last stitch to allow the beads to curve down.

Sew on the four red wooden beads, or glue on ⅜" red felt circles as indicated.

Hem the sides, if necessary, and hem the bottom. Add a fringe of the black yarn, using the method described on pages 85 and 163.

Fold the top over and hem, allowing room for rod. Slide in the rod. Put picture hooks or hooks for cafe rods in the wall spaced so that you can slip the ends of the rod into the picture hooks (Fig. 4).

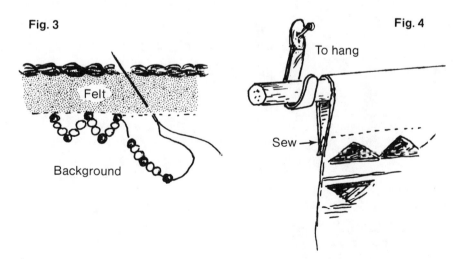

Fig. 3

Felt

Background

Fig. 4

To hang

Sew →

191

Sand Painting Plaque

Sand painting is an integral part of Navajo religious practice. These paintings — symbolic pictures made by trickling colored sand on the floor of the hogan — are made for a variety of rites concerning purification or healing. Each painting, completed just before the ceremony begins, is created specifically for that one occasion, after which it is destroyed. The total number of different designs the Navajos use is not known and no written or graphic records have been kept. The rituals have been handed down orally from generation to generation. Because of the sacred nature of the procedure, the Navajos have been traditionally unwilling to admit observers, but some watercolor and crayon copies of these paintings have been made. These are well documented and a good number of the copies have been done by the Navajo themselves.

There is no way really to recapture the original beauty and feeling of these sand paintings, but they can be inspirations for exciting designs for contemporary rooms.

The sand plaque described below results in a fascinatingly textured surface. It is not meant to copy sacred motifs. It could be decorated with any kind of design. If you feel this design is too complex, try other designs, using this technique. Decorate the plaque with a black mimbres bug (page 198), a sunflower, a bird or your own favorite symbol. The procedure is the same, whatever the subject.

MATERIALS

Sand; plaster of Paris; acrylic paints; burlap or chicken wire; wire for hangers; aluminum foil (optional); small and large paint brushes (preferably old); fiber brush (such as an old vegetable brush); colored sands or gravels (trade names: Chipstone, Textstone gravel, Crushed rock, Mosaic stone); white glue.

The background will be a plaster of Paris plaque cast in sand to give the natural sand surface. Gravel or colored sand is glued to this surface to create the design. These gravels are available to make textured, mosaic type pictures. Some toy stores carry them in kits. Craft supply stores usually have them by the bag. Get as fine a texture as possible, the nearest to sand, Aquarium gravel is too coarse. If you can't get all the colors desired, buy black and white, and use white as a substitute for the other colors, then paint these white areas with the other colors desired.

For a more subtle effect, the design can be made in sand you have colored yourself. Purchase fine sand (preferably white) sold for children's sandboxes (try toy stores). This sand has little dust and is fairly even-textured. Add a few drops of water to ¼ cup full strength liquid fabric dye. Imerse and soak sand in the dye. Spread dyed sand on newspapers and allow to dry.

To cast the plaque you'll need wet sand. A child's sandbox is good, or a natural beach. If you don't have access to these, purchase a bag of sand. Builder's supply and some handware stores carry sand by the bag for the use of homeowners in the winter to sand walks or to mix cement. The sterilized sand for sandboxes is more expensive but it is much more evenly textured.

Find a large corrugated box and line the bottom with foil. Fill with damp sand. Choose a box the size you want your plaque to be.

Make a flat indentation, build up the sides, packing the damp sand about 1¼ " high around edges (Fig. 1). Check to make sure that the flat area is set level.

To re-enforce the back, cut a piece of chicken wire, screening or burlap about 1" less all around than the dimension of plaque. For hangers, cut two pieces of sturdy wire, and attach them to the top of the chicken wire (Fig. 2).

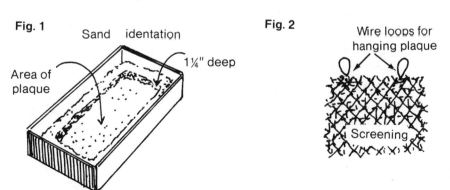

Fig. 1   Sand   identation

Area of plaque

1¼" deep

Fig. 2   Wire loops for hanging plaque   193

Screening

The casting is made of plaster of Paris which is available in most hardware stores. Spackling will also work. To mix, use a disposable paper bucket then discard bucket and leftover plaster. Never throw the mixture down the drain. Mix the plaster of Paris to a thick-cream consistency. To make the plaque a sand color, add some yellow or brown paint to tint the plaster for the first layer. Mix enough to make about a ¼ " layer on your bed of sand.

Pour the mixture into a corner of the indentation and allow the plaster of Paris to run across flat surface. It should be about ¼ " deep. The sand will be somewhat disturbed at the corner where you are pouring the plaster of Paris onto the "mold," so keep this slightly outside the contour of the plaque. It can be shaved off later with a knife.

Let this first layer set. When it is firm, repack the sand around the corner where you poured, reestablishing the contour of the plaque. Mix more plaster of Paris—without any coloring. Pour on, adding another ¼ " layer. Allow it to thicken, but before it sets completely, lay the wire reenforcement down into the plaster of Paris. The hanging wires should protrude above the edges of the plaque. Allow this layer to set.

Once more, mix another batch of plaster of Paris without any coloring and pour on, to cover any wire that may be showing. The overall finished depth of the plaque should be about ¾ ".

Pour each layer on after the previous one sets and is cool (it becomes warm when setting), but do not let it dry out between layers.

Allow the completed casting to dry overnight, then remove from the sand bed. Gently lift it up, brush off the excess sand and smooth the corner where the first layer was poured (Fig. 3). Continue brushing with a vegetable brush, removing the excess sand but leaving a sandy textured surface for the design.

Now that the plaque size is established, plan your design. Draw a figure inspired by Indian deities such as shown on page 196. Or make a simple one with just a bird, a sunflower or a frog. Enlarge one of the designs shown (for enlarging see page 12) or make your own. Keep the areas simple. Make notes of what color you plan for each area. From this drawing make a second drawing on brown wrapping paper or any scrap paper of the large major sections. Cut out these designs (Fig. 4). Place this pattern over your plaque. Dilute some black paint. With a brush go around the edge of the cut out areas, establishing the place-

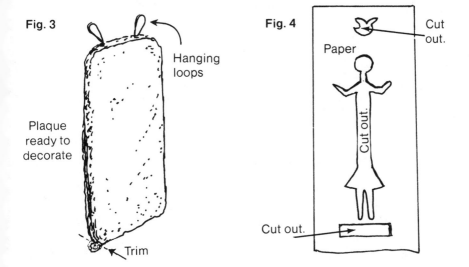

Fig. 3

Hanging
loops

Plaque
ready to
decorate

Trim

Fig. 4

Paper

Cut
out.

Cut out.

Cut out.

ment of the black areas of design. The paint should soak into the sand surface like a blotter; it should not leave a sharp painted edge. Repeat for white and colored areas by painting along edge of cut out with diluted white paint.

Remove the pattern and paint the remaining outlines free-hand, using your first drawing as a guide. Use black or white paint as needed. Paint should merely stain the surface as a guide for placing the gravel.

To glue on the colored gravel (or colored sand), put a little white glue in a dish, then thin it sufficiently with water so that it can be painted on with a brush. Brush glue over an area to be covered with a color. Take a handful of colored sand or gravel and sift it over the area you have brushed with wet glue. Do the same with the other areas of the same color. For fine lines, glue may be drizzled directly from cap of container if it can be evenly controlled. For small spots, dab the glue on with a small brush. Then pick up a pinch of sand between thumb and forefinger and drop it gently on the glued spot. Allow the glue to dry.

Place the plaque on old newspaper, tilt it up and gently tap off any excess gravel that has not stuck.

195

Apply the next color and repeat the process. When all the areas are filled with the proper color, go back and remove any color pieces that may be in the wrong place. Scratch off the pieces or pick them up

Fig. 5

Blue

Paint black over colored gravel.

with tweezers. Add more glue and fill in any places where the color texture is uneven or the color did not fill the design.

If you are doing the figure shown, to make mouth and eyes paint over the blue on the face with thinned black paint (Fig. 5). Other small details can be painted this way when they appear over colored gravel.

If you are using colored sand, some colors may not show sufficiently brightly against natural sand. To intensify the color, paint over each color with thinned acrylic paint. Make sure the paint does not obscure the texture of the sand or make any hard painted edges. The beauty of this painting is the sand textures against each other.

Allow everything to dry thoroughly. To ensure that the gravel stays in place, make a solution of half white glue, half water. With a large brush, gently drip and swish the glue over all colored areas. Do not disturb the surface. Allow to dry.

Hang on two sturdy picture hooks.

Bird

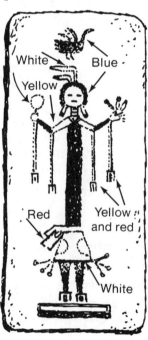

White

Blue

Yellow

Red

Yellow and red

White

Sunflower

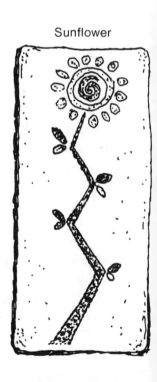

196

Mimbres Mirror

Pottery making has been practiced by many tribes for centuries. If you work with a kiln and wish to make ceramic pieces inspired by Indian shapes and designs, there is a wealth of material to choose from. Museums and art books are full of fine examples of decorated jugs, jars, bowls, etc. It would be hard *not* to be inspired.

Even if you don't work in pottery, such designs can be inspirations for other types of decoration.

Some of the most charming and whimsical creature designs were made long ago in the Mimbres valley of New Mexico. For centuries, pottery embellishments had been geometric shapes. Around 1,000 A.D., a new style appeared that continued for several centuries. This fresh new style added to the geometric motifs a great variety of creatures, mythical animals, insects, birds and men. Rendered in black and white, these creatures were depicted on shallow bowls in imaginative, witty, stylized designs.

The appeal of these stylized designs reaches across the centuries. A few are shown on the following page.

Pick a favorite design from those shown and decorate something with this motif. Paint it on a wall or on the cover of a box. Cut the shape out of adhesive-backed paper and stick it onto a book cover or mirror.

If you'd like to make several repeats of the same motif, a stencil is helpful. For instance, you might decorate a frame for a round mirror.

MATERIALS
Round mirror with cardboard frame; black, white (or tan) paint—preferably acrylic (poster paints will do); spray-on varnish; sponge; small brush; masking tape; 1½ yard black cord.

Many variety stores carry mirrors about 8″ in diameter with about 2″ of cardboard frame around the mirror. If you can't find such a mirror, use any round mirror and cut a cardboard frame. Make the inside circumference of the cardboard slightly smaller than the diameter of the mirror; make the outside circumference large enough to give a 2″ border to decorate.

Remove the cardboard from the mirror and paint it white (or tan).

MIMBRES MOTIFS

It may take several coats to cover the old design. Put the paint on thickly and bumpily.

To prepare the stencil, spray a piece of writing paper with spray-on varnish. When the varnish is dry, spray the other side and allow it to dry (or you can use as is the backing paper from adhesive type wall coverings).

To make the stencil, lay the prepared paper over the design chosen (such as the grasshopper). Trace the design onto the paper with a sharp pencil. Lay the paper on a scrap card, and cut out the design, using a knife or single edge razor blade. Leave the circle for the hole of the eye attached to the stencil (Fig. 1). The top of head will be painted in later. Make the stencil only of the large areas (Fig. 2)—the legs, antennae, and other fine lines will be filled in later.

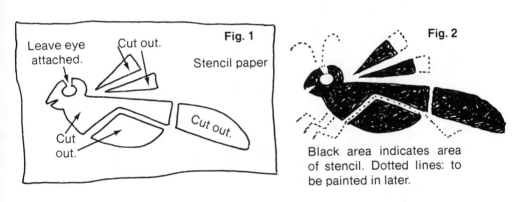

Fig. 1

Leave eye attached.

Cut out.

Stencil paper

Cut out.

Cut out.

Fig. 2

Black area indicates area of stencil. Dotted lines: to be painted in later.

To space the decorations on the mirror frame, draw a paper pattern of the frame. Divide it into six approximately even segments; or whatever number would best accommodate the repeat motif in the space to be decorated (Fig. 3). Lightly mark the segments on the cardboard. Tape the stencil in position on one segment.

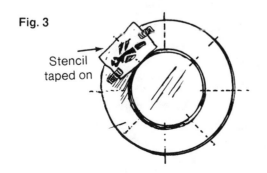

Fig. 3

Stencil taped on

To stencil, place black paint in a small dish—the paint should be fairly thick. Dip a sponge (or flat piece of foam rubber) into the paint. Dab it on scrap paper to be sure it transfers paint evenly. Then dab over the stencil. The paint should just barely cover the exposed area. A little texture of the background showing through is attractive.

To repeat, lift the stencil straight up. Be sure the stencil back has no wet paint on it. Tape the stencil to another segment and repeat. Continue until all the designs are in place. Acrylic dries fast, so keep adding moisture to the paint as needed, but keep it thick enough for sponging . . . and work fairly rapidly.

Complete the other portions of the motifs when the sponged-on areas are dry. With a fine brush, fill in the top of head, leaving the round white eye (Fig. 4). Add a dot in the center of the eye. Fill in the legs, antennae or whatever other details are needed.

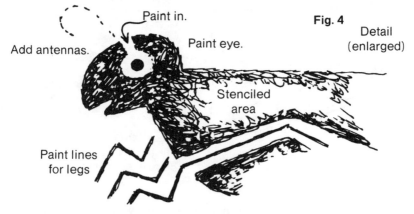

Add antennas.

Paint in.

Paint eye.

Fig. 4
Detail
(enlarged)

Stenciled
area

Paint lines
for legs

Spray the frame with varnish. When it is dry, glue the mirror back into position. For a finishing touch, glue black cord (or soutache braid or yarn) around the inner and outer edges of the frame (Fig. 5).

Fig. 5

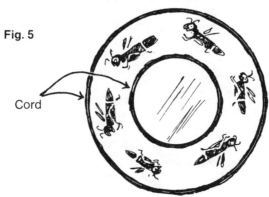

Cord

There are multitudes of uses for this technique and for the designs shown, depending on what and where you want decorations.

Dresser: Perk up a drab dresser. Repaint and stencil animal motifs down the drawers (Fig. 6).

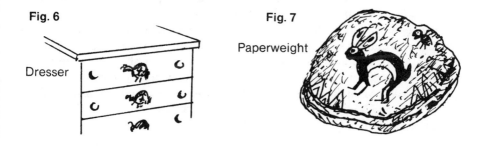

Fig. 6

Dresser

Fig. 7

Paperweight

Bulletin board: stencil designs around the edge of a bulletin board either on the frame or the cork.

Valance: enlarge the design to fit, cut stencils, paint.

Paperweight: make a bunch of rock weights if you've come across some fairly smooth whitish-colored rocks. Clean the rocks, stencil on the design (Fig. 7). Paint a black border, spray varnish.

Hand mirror: as these motifs were all orignally on round bowls they adapt especially well to round objects such as a small plastic hand mirror (Fig. 8). Remove old backing, paint a new one, insert in place. (Warm the plastic in hot water if you have trouble removing the backing).

Miscellaneous: with paint and stencils, you can rescue many objects: an old round box or a dingy metal bookend, for example (Fig. 9).

Fabric: these motifs can be stenciled on fabric with acrylic (see page 142). Once dry, acrylic will not wash out.

Fig. 8

Mirror

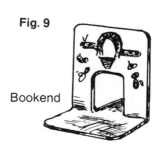

Fig. 9

Bookend

Birch Bark Belt Board

Birch bark had many uses for the Indians of the Northeast. They covered their homes as well as their canoes with it and made household articles from it. By folding, sewing the birchbark and caulking it with tar (like the canoe seams), containers of all kinds could be made waterproof. To decorate these birchbark vessels, the outer surface was scraped away, leaving a design of the rich, deep-brown under-surface. Sometimes the designs were familiar animals of the area, but often these designs had graceful curves suggesting plant forms.

Surely such an indigenous craft as birch bark carving should inspire a contemporary concoction. How about something practical? If you've been making belts, jewelry or such, you probably now have quite a collection tangled up in drawers and boxes. The purpose of this "birchbark" board is to hang them in style, tanglefree.

MATERIALS

Wooden board about 4¾" x 15" x ½" thick; piece of cardboard 4¾" x 15"; white tissue paper; white glue; walnut furniture stain; brown paint (acrylic, latex or oil); two screw-on type hanging rings; six large cup hooks (brown or brass); old brush; sandpaper.

Sand the board smooth and stain it deep brown, following the directions on the can of stain.

For surfacing to simulate the bark texture, tissue will be crumpled, then glued to cardboard and motifs cut out. The cardboard then will be attached to the wood.

Cut the cardboard exactly the same size as the wooden board.

To apply the tissue: thin the white glue—½ glue to ½ water. Cut some strips of tissue paper about 5" x 2". Lay the cardboard on a piece of scrap paper. Brush on a layer of the thinned glue. Lay a strip of tissue on the cardboard, wrinkling the tissue as you go. Accordian pleat the tissue, in irregular patterns into the glue. It should create crumpled vertical lines as it adheres to the cardboard (Fig. 1). Brush

PATTERN

Cut out all areas
indicated in grey

Top

Center
motif

Center line; fold, trace for other side.

203

the thinned glue on top and under as you apply pieces of tissue, thoroughly saturating the tissue. Cover the entire cardboard piece and allow it to dry. Trim off the excess along edges.

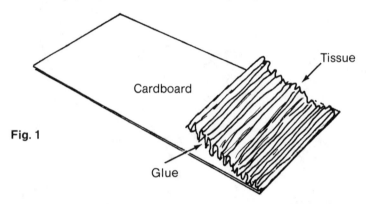

Fig. 1

Trace the design for one half of the board (see pattern on page 203) on a piece of tracing paper 4¾″ x 15″. Fold the paper and trace the motif for the other half. Open up. After tracing the design, transfer it to the back of the tissued cardboard. With a knife (or single edge razor blade—please be careful), cut out the design. The center units will come out, but don't discard them (Fig. 2), they will be assembled later into the design. Trim all the edges neatly and give the front and cut edges a coat of the thinned glue.

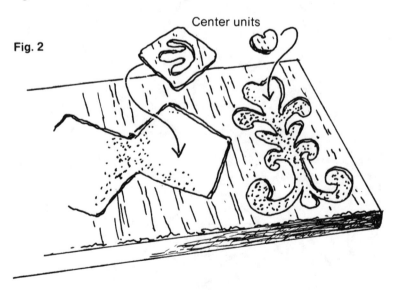

Fig. 2

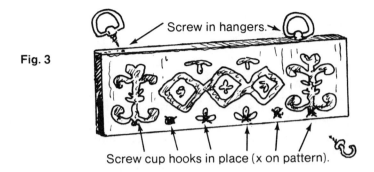

Fig. 3

Screw in hangers.

Screw cup hooks in place (x on pattern).

When the cardboard piece is dry, give the *board* a coat of full strength glue. Lay on the cardboard (with design cut in it), tissue side up. Place the center motifs in position (Fig. 2). The dark brown wood now shows through to create the design. Weight down the cardboard and allow the glue to dry.

To seal the edges so the final stain won't run under, give the unit a coat of thinned glue over both the board and design.

When this coat of glue is thoroughly dry, brush the stain over the board, covering the white areas. Allow the stain to set briefly, then gently wipe it, watching the effect as you wipe. The surfaces should be a light tan with dark brown in the valleys of the tissue wrinkles. It should look something like a sophisticated old antique, with a birch bark effect. If you wipe too much, the effect may be lost. Brush on more stain and try again. Make sure that the finished color of the tissued area is light enough for the design to show but dark enough to achieve desired texture.

When the stain is dry, paint the edges of the wood and cardboard. When the paint is dry, screw hangers (Fig. 3) in the top of the board. Space the six hooks along the bottom about ½" from the edge. Screw in position. Hang the board on a wall and display your liveliest paraphernalia. Hang belts, pendants etc., on the cup hooks.

This technique is useful for many other items. You might restore an old wooden box by staining top brown. Draw a design to fit (Fig. 4) and cut the tissued cardboard. Glue to top.

Fig. 4

Little Accents

Basket Weaving

One of the oldest crafts on this continent is basket weaving. By the time the Europeans arrived, basketry in many areas was a fine art. Especially in the Northwest and Southwest, fine intricate baskets were woven. A variety of weaving techniques were used and many had woven-in designs. Some baskets were so tightly woven that they could hold water and others were constructed so that they could be used for cooking.

The double strand weave produces a strong, durable basket. Cane and reed are usually used but maybe you'd like to start with a substitute. If you have an old plastic reed curtain around, you can use it to practice weaving and get the feel of the technique.

MATERIALS

Valance of plastic reeds (brown or color preferred); twisted raffia of contrasting color, available in craft supply stores (or wrapping twine or jute or other cords sold for macramé); 14 wooden beads approx. ½" diameter (optional).

When making a basket, the verticals that are woven *onto* are called "stakes." For this basket you use the plastic reeds from a valance. Separate about 30 reeds from the valance by cutting the connecting threads. Crisscross six across each other (Fig. 1). Flatten them slightly if necessary. Tie them at the center point (or glue them if desired). When the glue is dry, you may start weaving. Cut two strands of cord (raffia) about 30" or 36" long. Pass these two weaving strands ("weavers") around either side of each stake, alternating each time (Fig. 2). Tighten and push down. Go around and around.

After spiraling around making a woven circle about 1" diameter, start adding new stakes. Poke new ones into the furrows created by the existing stakes (Fig. 3). As you weave around, treat each new stake separately and soon it will create its own furrow.

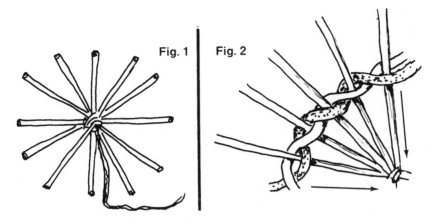

Fig. 1

Fig. 2

Weave another ½″, then add another row of new stakes in alternate rows around.

When the weaving cord begins to run out, add a new length of cord by weaving it double with the old cord for a few turns to make sure it will hold. As you push the weaving down the new cord will be secured (Fig. 4).

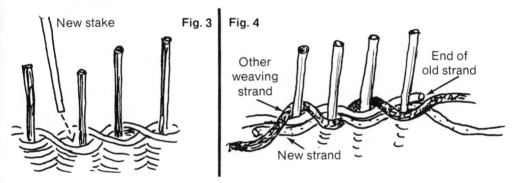

New stake

Fig. 3

Fig. 4

Other weaving strand

End of old strand

New strand

After you have woven a flat disk about 4″ across, set the disk over your knee or an appropriately shaped pot and bend each stake to create the basket shape (Fig. 5). Continue weaving, now establishing the vertical sides of the basket. Adjust the tension of the weaving to hold this shape.

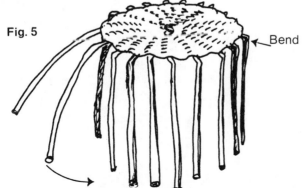

Fig. 5

Bend

As the original stakes begin to get too short, add new ones in the furrows before the old ones are finished (Fig. 3). By this time you should have almost all the stakes you need in place, if not, keep adding them as before.

If the stakes tend to pull out when you weave, add a bit of white glue to the tip of the stake when you insert it. When the glue dries, continue weaving.

For an interesting effect, after you have about woven 2½" up the sides, slip a large wooden bead over every other stake. There *should* be an even number of stakes. Weave up another ¾" above beads.

To finish the top, cut the stakes about 2" above the last row of weaving (Fig. 6). Bend each stake sharply to the left and insert into the weave-furrow of the second stake over (Fig. 7). If necessary use the tip of a knitting needle or similar tool to open up enough space in furrow top to slip the stake end in. Continue around the top, bending and inserting the end of each stake in the furrow of the second stake over.

Fig. 6   **Fig. 7**

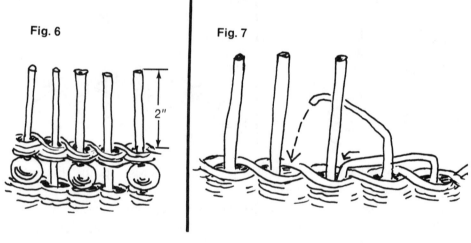

2″

This should be firm and make a neat finish around the top. If you wish to make the ends more secure, take a single strand of your weaving material and thread it on a large-eyed blunt needle. Go around the top, making two passes around each set of folded over stakes (Fig. 8).

This basket can be varied considerably in height and width. Use two colors for weaving cords if you like. Or go up about 2″ with one color, and then change both weavers to make a band of contrasting color.

Make the shape of the basket rounder and flatter for a letter basket. Make the basket larger in all directions and you've got a wastebasket. Use plastic reed cafe curtains about 18″ long to make the stakes for a wastebasket.

Fig. 8

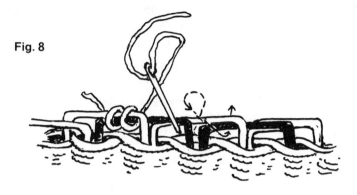

Pencil Holder (inspired by quillwork)

The ancient art of porcupine quillwork is truly indigenous—only the Indians of North America made quillwork. The process was long and tedious. The quills had to be soaked to make them flexible and were generally dyed as well. In woven quillwork threads were sewn to fabric or leather and the quills were worked in and out as the threads were sewn down. After beads became available, the art was virtually lost. Quillwork can never be imitated, but its color and design can be an inspiration for contemporary crafts.

MATERIALS

Needlepoint canvas about 7″ x 12″ small can about 3½″ high 2″ diameter (such as broiled mushrooms come in); rayon straw (trade names: "Hi-straw," "Swiss straw," "Ribbon Straw," etc.) in tan, red, blue or any color combination you prefer, fabric glue; tapestry needle; piece of leather (or felt) large enough to line the can.

Choose the can size you prefer for a pencil holder. Wash and dry the can.

To make the pattern, plan a design, such as the one shown (Fig. 1a).

Determine the size your design will need to be by measuring the height and circumference of your can. On a piece of paper, draw these dimensions and then plan a design to cover using large geometric motifs. Transfer the key lines of this design to the needle point canvas (Fig. 1B). Draw the top and bottom edge of each stripe, the points of the triangles, etc. Using a magic marker, follow the threads of the canvas as you draw in the lines. Allow some extra canvas all around the pattern for holding while working.

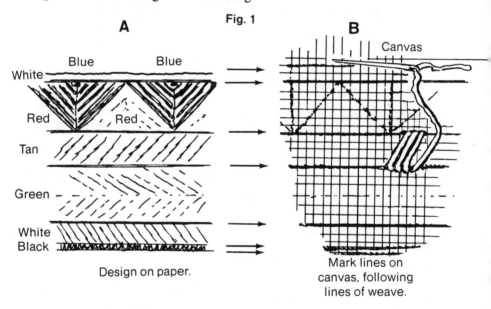

Fig. 1

A

Design on paper.

B

Mark lines on canvas, following lines of weave.

To work the design, thread a length of straw in needle. Tie a knot in the end of the straw. Work the motif by coming up from the back of the canvas, stitching across at an angle to the other side of pattern. Go straight down into the canvas again, coming back up in the next hole (Fig. 2). Stitch back across the canvas into the hole next to the one you came up in originally. Sew the straw down into the hole, come back up in the next hole, etc. Sew all the stitches evenly, without pulling, one right next to the other, following the lines of the canvas (Fig. 3).

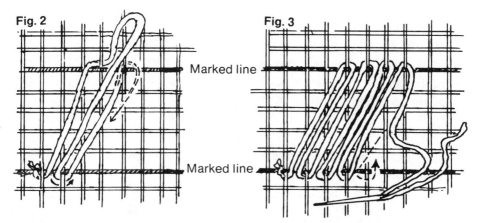

Fig. 2

Fig. 3

Marked line

Marked line

This is the basic procedure. Some stitches will angle across two squares of canvas, some across three. You can vary the width of each bar of color, by varying the number of rows of the canvas that each bar covers.

Once you get the principle of the technique, it is easy to use. You can then adapt the design to fit the size and shape of the canvas you want to cover or you can create your own designs.

When completed, trim the canvas near the straw work (Fig. 4), being careful to leave enough canvas to hold all stitches in place. Dab fabric glue along the edges of the canvas and fold the edges back under the worked canvas, so that no unworked canvas shows. Weight down the canvas and allow it to dry.

To line the can, trace around its base on the back of a piece of leather. For base, cut out a circle of leather slightly smaller in circumference. For sides, measure the height of the can, and add 1". Measure the diameter of can. Cut a rectangular piece of leather to these dimensions. Fit the piece of leather down inside of the can. Mark where the pieces overlap. Remove the leather from the can. Trim the edges of the leather so the ends will butt inside. Fold down the top of the leather ½" (Fig. 5). Glue the leather circle inside the base of the can and glue the lining around the inside of the can. Glue the ½" foldover to the outside of the can.

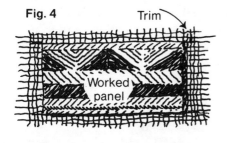

Fig. 4   Trim

Worked panel

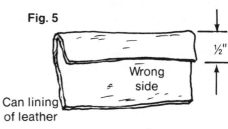

Fig. 5

½"

Wrong side

Can lining of leather

211

When the glue is dry, glue the straw-worked piece around the can, butting the ends in back (Fig. 6). Overlap the straw over the leather edge slightly. Hold the straw piece closed with clip clothespins and rubber bands until the glue is dry. Glue a piece of felt the same size as the base under bottom of the can.

If you prefer you can make just a small panel to decorate the bottom of the can. Spray the can with colorful paint. Glue a narrow strip of leather around the top. Glue a straw panel at the bottom (Fig. 7).

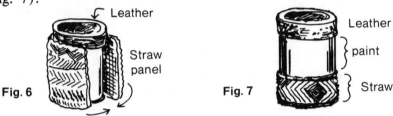

Fig. 6 — Leather / Straw panel

Fig. 7 — Leather / paint / Straw

If you enjoy working with this material, try making a variety of accessories. Do the corners of a desk pad, or a letter basket. Make an eyeglass case, line it with felt. For a belt, sew or glue a straw-worked piece to a leather or fabric belt. Make square coasters, by gluing a square of straw to felt. There are forms sold with the plastic straw material to make round coasters.

Assemblage — A Natural Family

Sand painting; detail (Navaho)

This last project assumes that you have been inspired to try some projects of your own, and that you now have accumulated various odds and ends of of leather and wood pieces.

Some figures in this assemblage have round, others square, heads. It is interesting to note that in paintings of deities of certain Southwestern tribes, the female was shown with a square head, the male with the round. For our purposes, a variation in shapes gives interest to the sculpture.

MATERIALS

A variety of wooden dowels, balls, cubes, etc.; for the base: a piece of driftwood about ½" x ½" x 12" (or wood piece); scraps of suede leather; chamois; a few tiny feathers; assortment of seed and "real" beads; fine sandpaper; white glue; fabric glue; teak stain; masking tape; beading wire; hand saw.

The drawing on page 215 shows an arrangement approximately half size. This is only a suggestion for the assortment of sizes, the placement of figures and for decorations. Naturally you will make it with whatever you find available.

For the large round heads, use unpainted wooden balls or knobs, 1" or 1½" diameter, which are generally available. The square rods, cubes and some of the round dowels might be found in a bag of wood pieces sold at a lumber yard, or in a child's building toy set, (with natural finish). Look in workshop scraps, wood trims, anywhere there might be pieces with potential use.

For the smallest round heads, use wooden beads in a natural color. Wooden dowels in varying diameters are best for the round bodies.

Painted pieces can be used if you are ambitious and sand off all the paint. The natural finish is part of the beauty of this sculpture. An old broomstick, sanded, is a good size for the body of the biggest round figure.

Pile together your collection of pieces. See what fits in size and shape. Determine what length bodies are needed to fit the heads available. Mark this length on dowels or sticks. With a saw, cut them to the proper lengths. Keep restacking pieces until you have a selection of sizes and shapes which will make the most pleasing arrangement. Some should be taller, some fatter. Each should be different in height and diameter. Place square heads on round dowels, round heads on square rods.

On a piece of paper, make a diagram of your stacks so you will

213

remember the exact placement. Draw your arrangement actual size so it looks something like diagram shown.

Sand all the pieces. Brush on stain to give the piece a mellow color. Wipe the stain off as directed on can of stain.

For the base of the assemblage, trim the driftwood if it needs it and sand the top so there are flat spots on which to stand the figures. If you are using a piece of wood, round the edges slightly and sand them smooth. Stain the base also, if necessary.

Glue the heads to the bodies as planned in the diagram. Hold the pieces together with masking tape until the glue is dry (Fig. 1). Beads with holes should be positioned so that holes are vertical.

On your diagram decide where the trim will go. Plan where to add tiny scraps of leather for loincloths, a cape, etc. Decide where beading will add a touch of color. Cut paper patterns of the leather shapes to determine exact size. Cut strips of paper and fit them around the "heads" for headbands.

When you have made all the patterns and tested them for size, use them to cut the pieces out of a variety of colors and weights of leather, suede and chamois.   Using fabric glue, attach the pieces   as planned.

One of the headbands is soft chamois. Wet the chamois, wrap it around the head, gathering it slightly. Lap the ends over each other and let them hang down. Glue it in this position. Hold the headband with tape until the glue is dry (Fig. 2).

For legging fringe, cut chamois strips about ½" wide and in the length needed. Cut a ¼" fringe along the entire length of the chamois.

214

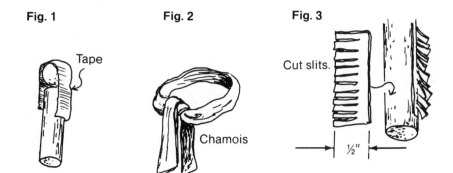

Fig. 1 Tape

Fig. 2 Chamois

Fig. 3 Cut slits. ½"

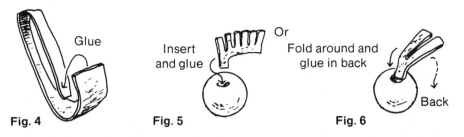

Glue

Fig. 4

Insert and glue

Or

Fold around and glue in back

Back

Fig. 5

Fig. 6

Wet the chamois and glue it onto the side of dowel, shaping the fringe downward so that it will dry in that position (Fig. 3).

The bandolier bag is a leather strip with one end slightly wider than the other. Glue the ends of the strip together, the wider end on the outside, as shown. Glue the leather strip around and down the side of the dowel figure (Fig. 4). Add some beads if desired.

Where wooden beads are used as heads, there is a hole in the top. You can stick feathers in some of the holes. Others can be filled with leather to look like hair or a roach. Cut a piece of chamois as shown (Fig. 5). Glue along the edge and poke the long end into the hole,

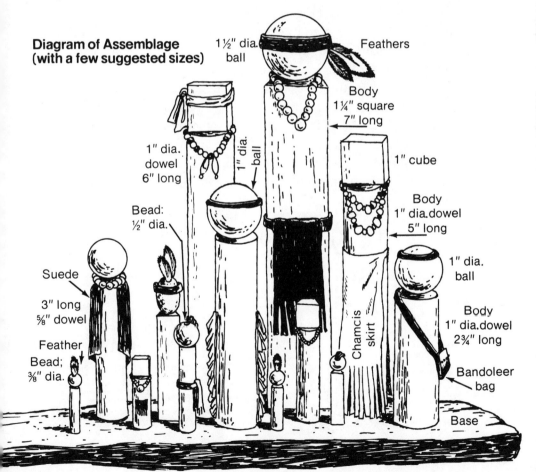

Diagram of Assemblage (with a few suggested sizes)

1½" dia. ball

Feathers

Body 1¼" square 7" long

1" cube

1" dia. dowel 6" long

1" dia. ball

Body 1" dia. dowel 5" long

Bead: ½" dia.

Suede

1" dia. ball

3" long ⅝" dowel

Body 1" dia. dowel 2¾" long

Feather Bead; ⅜" dia.

Chamcis skirt

Bandoleer bag

Base

pressing the fringe down along the back of the head.

For bead decorations, string assorted beads on beading wire. The taller figures can wear large beads. Use the tiniest beads on the little figures. After stringing the beads, twist the wire in back and glue. Apply the glue with a toothpick if necessary. When the glue is dry, clip the wire ends and shape the wire so that the beads hang well in front.

Don't overdo the beadwork, five or six figures with beads are plenty. Have the bead assortment blend with the wood if possible; use yellow and orange beads, brown and tans, off white, etc. The whole sculpture should be in mellow, natural tones.

When all pieces are ready, glue each piece to the base following your diagram. Put white glue on the underside of piece, use strips of masking tape around the base (Fig. 6) and press it down. Press the tape around the board or driftwood to hold the pieces in position while the glue is drying (Fig. 7). Glue on as many of the large pieces as possible. Allow the glue to dry. Remove the tape. Glue on the rest of the large figures and the small ones, using the same technique. Allow the glue to dry.

Glue feathers in the holes planned (if you have a parakeet or a canary, you can use the feathers you find on the bottom of the cage.) Two or three figures with feathers are sufficient. Use your judgment for placement and color.

Your silent family is complete. Set it on a shelf or coffee table to remind you of the heritage of this continent and "Indian Inspirations."

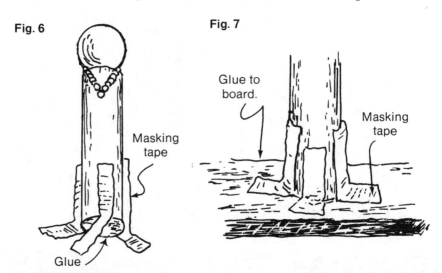

Fig. 6

Masking tape

Glue

Fig. 7

Glue to board.

Masking tape

Masking tape

⹁Using Craft Techniques

Added Ideas

Throughout the book a number of craft techniques have been discussed, techniques that can now be adapted for your household or for gifts. Here are a few suggestions:

As described in Chapter I, beading, both applied and loomed, can transform many mundane but useful articles into something fashionable and fun to keep. Look around, what drab little things might become visual delights with some help?

BEADWORK

Eyeglass case: Add a beaded band to an eyeglass case. Trace the pattern from a case on hand, cut the pieces of felt or leather. Glue or sew on beadwork, then sew up sides. Or bead a felt panel and glue over a commercial case.

Box, etc.: Glue a beaded circle to the top of a pill box (Fig. 1). Sew a band around an umbrella case or handle. Transform a small can into a pencil holder by gluing a beaded panel around it.

Fig. 1

Beaded
rosette

Beadwork

METAL AND SHELL

Boxes, frames, etc.: Tooled metal or shell arrangements, described for jewelry, could also be used for decorating objects. Make in the proper size to decorate the top of a small box (Fig. 2). Inlay a box top. Add shells and beads to the corners of a mirror frame (Fig. 3) or use tooled metal cut to fit (Fig. 4). Cut and shape a bone piece to make a letter opener.

Fig. 2

Embossed
Copper

Fig. 3

Glue flat shells in corners, loose strands of beads between, and loose hanging beads on each side.

Fig. 4

Embossed copper shapes of hands: decorative sun Glue to old mirror frame.

217

Fabric ideas in Chapter II and III are very adaptable for house adornments. Think of all the household objects that use fabric, then imagine all that can be crafted.

SEMINOLE PIECEWORK

In large or small sections, this piecework can be very effective.

Potholder: Start small, piece a potholder (Fig. 5). Make two 7″ squares, pad inside with a square of art-foam or terrycloth, bind edges. There you have a unique gift! Think even smaller, fill a tiny square with fragrant powder, and you have a sachet.

Pillow: For a square throw pillow, make a pieced strip down the middle, plain fabric on each side to make the square (Fig. 6). Fit and sew to a purchased pillow form. Or cut a plain pillow back to match the front, bind edges and stuff.

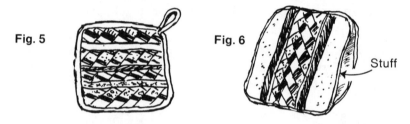

Fig. 5   Fig. 6   Stuff

Bordering: Now you are ready for anything (Fig. 7). Make a pieced border to edge everything or anything: placemats, seat covers, curtains, tablecloth—or even edge a bedspread if you're ambitious.

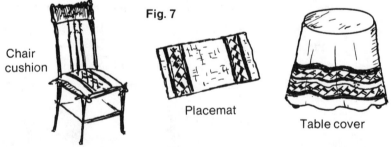

Fig. 7

Chair cushion

Placemat

Table cover

Comforter: For the *very* ambitious, a bedcover or comforter could be assembled of piecework sections, alternating with plain fabric squares (Fig. 8). Line with plain cotton fabric. For warmth, add cotton batt sold for quilts (or use an old blanket). Pin quilt top and cotton batt to lining and stitch through all three at corners of each square to hold flat. Bind edges.

Fig. 8

Fabric square
Piecework
Cotton batt
Lining

WEAVING

Weaving has many possibilities, even using the small crude loom described. Make placemats, a pillow cover, seat covers.

Coaster: Weave small squares for unique coasters. Leave ends of both warp and weft. Sew around edges to keep from raveling (Fig. 9).

Rug: Weave with rug yarn as weft, sturdy twine for warp. Make sections as large as your loom allows. Sew pieces together with yarn for a small scatter rug. Add fringes (Fig. 10).

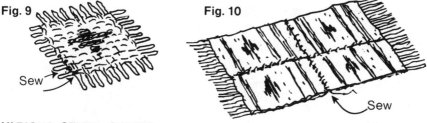

Fig. 9

Sew

Fig. 10

Sew

VARIOUS OTHER CRAFTS

Napkins: Stamping (as described for scarfs on page 142) can transform plain fabrics. Choose a design and stamp decorative corners and borders on a set of napkins or fabric placemats.

Hotplate: The basketry technique described for the woven sandal is a very practical technique for other things. Make a hotplate using jute to wrap around the clothesline in colors that glow. Start with a center fold of clothesline about 2″ long. Keep going until hotplate is a practical size. For coasters, weave small rounds using this method.

Think about what you have read and made. To make gifts or to enhance your home, add your own individuality and talents to the ideas here. Your finished product may still retain its Indian inspired feeling or have a completely contemporary look—what is important—it is your own creation.

219

Conclusion

This book has only suggested some possibilities for Indian inspirations. We hope you have now read the introduction to each craft and have tried your hand at one of the projects, at least. Time and patience can perfect any craft, so keep at it. Whatever your interest and aptitudes, there should be a craft for you somewhere in this book.

Inspirations are everywhere, in museums, books, all kinds of stores, in nature—you can develop an eye to recognize them. Indian craftsmanship can be more fully appreciated after working a few crafts of your own. Only by doing, can you truly understand the patience and skill of others.

With the ideas in this book, you can create objects to suit any fad or fancy that may arise. Basic craft techniques, once learned, can always be utilized. Watch the boutiques and ads for ideas that are current. With a little ingenuity you can make any accessory. As you become increasingly proficient with various techniques, eventually you may find yourself setting new trends. Have the courage of your convictions, taste and talent.

Design for the future—inspired by techniques as old as man. We hope that "Indian Inspirations" will inspire you to reexamine your country's heritage at the same time it inspires you to explore your own creative abilities.

Suppliers

Most of the supplies you will need can be found in local craft, hobby or art stores. Fake fur is available by the yard (in season) in fabric shops. Most hardware stores and craft suppliers carry dowels. Small decorative feathers can be found in shops for fishermen who tie their own flies. Many local stores (such as Woolworths) carry a variety of craft materials such as remnants of fake fur, beads, yarns and other such craft supplies.

Be creative in seeking materials. Try second hand shops and garage sales. Old hand bags or a jacket may be a good source of leather. Select those with adequate areas of usable leather. Old jewelry may yield appropriate beads to incorporate in your creations. You might find some shells if you have access to a beach.

Below are some mail order suppliers who carry special materials.

SAX ARTS AND CRAFTS: 2405 S. Calhoun Rd., New Berlin, WI 53151 (Catalog $4.00)
  • *Copper shapes and other craft supplies*

SUNCOAST Discount Arts and Crafts: 9015 US Hwy 19 North, Pinellas Park, FL 34666 (Catalog $2.00)
  • *Feathers, leather lacing, wood shapes, jewelry findings and other craft supplies*

VETERAN LEATHER CO. INC: 204 25th St. Brooklyn, NY 11232 (Catalog $2.00)
  • *Leather, moccasin kits, lacing and related materials*

WAKEDA TRADING POST: P.O. Box 19146, Sacramento CA 95819
  • *Beads (large selection), abalone pieces, fur, bone beads, button blanket beads and many other Indian craft supplies*

ZIMMERMANS: 2884-34 St North, St. Petersburg, FL 33713 (Catalog $2.00)
  • *Beads, yarn and other craft supplies*

SIOUX TRADING POST: 913 Mt. Rushmore Rd., Rapid City, SD 57701 (Catalog $2.00)
  • *Beads, moccasins, abalone*

TANDY CRAFT: Stores nationwide. See your local phone book for addresses or write 1001 Foch St., Fort Worth, TX 76107
  • *Leather, thongs, moccasin kits, feathers, prebeaded pieces and beads*

Index

223